ABOVE THE LINE

URBAN MEYER

ABOVE THE LINE

LESSONS IN LEADERSHIP AND LIFE
FROM A CHAMPIONSHIP SEASON

with Wayne Coffey

PENGUIN PRESS
NEW YORK
2015

PENGUIN PRESS
An imprint of Penguin Random House LLC
375 Hudson Street
New York, New York 10014
penguin.com

Photograph credits appear on pages 251–52.

Diagrams by Focus 3. Used by permission.

ISBN 978-1-101-98070-5

Printed in the United States of America
9   10   8

DESIGNED BY AMANDA DEWEY

All of the author's proceeds from the book will
go to the Urban and Shelley Meyer Family Foundation.

To my amazing wife of twenty-six years, Shelley,
and to our three incredible children,
Nicki, Gigi, and Nate.

CONTENTS

||||||||||||||||||||||||||||||

ABOVE THE LINE

PROLOGUE: LEADING FROM THE HEART

||||||||||||||||||||||||||||||||||||

T he book you are holding contains my thoughts and reflections on life and leadership. It is a compendium of what I've learned in more than a quarter-century of coaching, a real-life leadership manual that offers insights and information into what we did in the 2014 season that culminated in winning the first-ever College Football Playoff National Championship.

The defining characteristic of every championship team is leadership. Leadership isn't *a* difference maker, it is *the* difference maker. Talent will get you about seven or eight wins. Discipline pushes it to nine wins, maybe. But when you add leadership, that's when magic happens.

I've come to learn that leadership is not automatically granted to you because of your position or your salary or the size of your office. Leadership is influence based on trust that you have earned. A leader is not someone who declares what he wants and then gets angry when he doesn't get it. A true leader is someone who is going someplace and taking people with him, a catalyst for elite performance who enables people to achieve things they wouldn't achieve on their own. A leader is someone who earns trust, sets a clear standard, and then equips and inspires people to meet that standard.

I've learned that talent cannot replace leadership. There is a long line of teams full of talented players and coaches who fail to produce results equal to their talent. Leaders take teams beyond talent to a place they likely thought was unreachable. It doesn't happen by accident. It happens because coaches and players are willing to respond to the everyday challenge of leadership. Nothing can stop the team that harnesses the power of leadership. Nothing can help the team that doesn't.

Over the years, I have grown as a leader. I've made mistakes, and I've learned from those mistakes. I've had great mentors in men such as Earle Bruce, Lou Holtz, Sonny Lubick, and Bob Davie, and the lessons I've learned from them I carry with me to this day. To me, it's all about getting better. I am a long, long way from perfect, but I will put my passion for self-improvement next to anybody's. Maybe the only thing that rivals that in my makeup is the distaste I have for losing.

It has been that way since I was a kid in northeast Ohio, where one of my early lessons was that eight miles is a very long way to run. It's longer still if you are wearing a full baseball uniform and you've completely let your team down, losing a ball game because your bat never left your shoulder. I had to run. I had to do something. I'd just stood there with the game on the line, star shortstop turned statue, as useless as a freighter stuck on the shoals of nearby Lake Erie. This was my senior year at St. John High School in my hometown of Ashtabula. It was early May 1982, a beautiful spring day until the end of it. I was about to get drafted by the Atlanta Braves, sign for a whopping $13,000 bonus, and go off to play a couple of forgettable years of professional baseball, but for the moment I was still a St. John Herald, with the tying and winning runs on base in a one-run game against our archrival, Harbor High School.

I love rivalry games. I loved them then and might love them even more now. No regular-season game on the Ohio State football schedule is bigger than when we play "That Team Up North" (it begins with M, but Woody Hayes taught us never to say the name around Columbus). The Harbor pitcher was a kid named John Light. He was good. He threw hard and had a great knuckleball. There were two outs in the bottom of the seventh inning. It was all on me, just the way I liked it. I got behind in the count and on a 2–2 pitch I knew that John Light was coming with a knuckleball or curve. He'd never come right at me, not in this spot. Except this time he did, a fastball down the middle, belt high, over the heart of the plate. It might as well have had a little sign on it that said CRUSH ME. No kidding. It was that fast. But I never budged. I just froze. The ump rang me up, and the pitch was so perfect I couldn't even turn around and say, "Are you kidding me?"

The ump would've told me to shut up and try swinging next time.

Some people had the idea that my father, Bud Meyer, a tough guy who was old school even by old school standards, ordered me to run home as punishment for coming up small. My father was not beyond doing that; one time when I was in third grade and getting into some mischief in Mrs. Stofko's class, she asked my dad how he wanted her to handle it.

"Paddle him. Use a ruler. Punish him any way you want," my father said.

Mrs. Stofko said she couldn't do that without a parent's written permission. So my father immediately signed a note, giving her permission. Mrs. Stofko kept the note in the drawer. It was amazing how fast my behavior improved.

Another time, my little sister, Erika, was getting bullied at school. I think she was in first grade, and this kid wouldn't leave her alone. My father told me I needed to take care of the situation—to protect the family at all costs. The next day, I saw the kid at school, and, as directed by my father, I punched him in the face. I was in third grade. It was the first punch I'd ever thrown. I got sent to the principal's office, but I was a hero to my father. He took us out to eat at a place called the Swallows, on the corner of West and Prospect, an old brick place with a checkerboard tile floor, right behind the movie theater. "You sit at the head of the table," my father told me. "You're a man now. Family is everything."

The run home had nothing to do with my father, though. It had completely to do with how much I hate to lose and how upset I was that I had let the team down. The concept of team, of committed, hardworking athletes bonding together for a greater purpose, has always been sacred to me. You are going to read a lot in this book about team and about ideas such as small-unit cohesion, 10-80-10, the R Factor, and the Performance Pathway. You're going to read about how to build a winning culture in your organization and how to get your people to buy in. All of it is driven by a mission to lead people to achieve exceptional things. It takes an enormous amount of work, but the payoff is worth it because there's no better feeling in sports than seeing a group of young men give selflessly and work tirelessly to make the team the priority. Remarkable things happen when that occurs. Championships happen.

The Ohio State University's victory in the first College Football Playoff title game happened.

Let me tell you about a young man named Nik Sarac. Unless you are a serious Ohio State Buckeye fan, you've probably never heard of him. Nik is a five-foot nine-inch, 183-pound defensive back from Saint Ignatius High School in Cleveland, a kid who walked on in 2011 and spent the next four years working as hard as any player I've ever coached. Nik wasn't blessed with great physical ability, but he's going to be a great doctor someday, and I'd compare his makeup, his commitment to the team, and his drive to get better with anybody's. He never missed a regular-season practice in four years. Not one. And talk about selflessness: After Nik's junior year, I decided I was going to give him a scholarship, and I called him and his father to tell them. The example Nik set and the way he went about his work and cared about his teammates made it entirely deserved. It meant a lot to Nik to be a scholarship player; it was the ultimate validation of him as an OSU football player.

And you know what he did? He turned the scholarship down. He said his family could afford to pay for his final season.

"Save it for somebody who really needs it," Nik said.

Wow.

I'm not often speechless, but I was then. It was one of the most unselfish things I've ever seen a kid—or anybody else—do. Later I found out Nik had a major role in helping one of his teammates through some serious stresses in his school and family life. The kid was lost and overwhelmed and decided to walk away from the team. Maybe more than anybody else, Nik was there for him, working him through the difficulties, letting him know how much he cared. The kid eventually came back, and with a recharged focus and commitment. He is in a much better place now. I can't prove it, but I bet it wouldn't have happened without Nik. When we had our celebration in Ohio Stadium the Saturday after the victory over Oregon in January 2015, I called Nik out of the bleachers and introduced him. All of his teammates started chanting his name: "Sarac! Sarac! Sarac!" Nik Sarac will never play a down in the NFL. He will probably never be on ESPN or mentioned when people talk about Buckeye greats. But let me tell you something. Nik Sarac was as important to our team as Ezekiel Elliott, Cardale Jones, Joey Bosa, Jeff Heuerman, Curtis Grant, Joshua Perry, Devin Smith, or anybody else.

Nik was a glue guy, a team guy, a guy who never, ever

stopped putting out, and everybody on the team knew it. I love that kid. Everybody on the team loves him. It is impossible not to. All he ever did was work and care. Nik played in seven games in four years. The marching band was on the field more than he was. It didn't matter. He gave everything he had to the team, including his scholarship. We will have a place for a kid like that for as long as I am a coach.

While there are some timeless truths about leadership, there are also different styles and approaches. What works for Bob Stoops or Bill Belichick might not work for me, and vice versa. If I've learned one thing, it's that you have to be true to yourself. You can't be one way on Monday and another way on Tuesday. Earle Bruce, the former Ohio State coach, taught me that early on. As head coach, you are the guy who ultimately calls the shots. You are also the emotional and spiritual leader, the guy who sets the direction for the team and shows the way. You will not be successful as a leader if you are constantly changing directions.

Another thing I've learned is that if you think you know it all, you are setting yourself up for a major fall. Jon Gruden has reminded me many times: "Don't sleep on the game of football; it'll sneak up and bite you." I think this applies way beyond the football field, and so does most everything else we're going to talk about in this book. Leaders are learners. I want to learn as much as I can today and then do it again tomorrow. I probably learned more in the 2014 season than I have in my entire coaching career. And I learned the most from our players and our coaches. I love to ask questions and seek ways to make our team better every day. I believe that this kind of curiosity and drive are two of the greatest qualities a leader can have. Look at people like Phil Knight, Dan Gilbert, and the late Steve Jobs. Look at the leadership team at ESPN. All of these people and their companies keep pushing, innovating, and improving. Is it risky at times? Sure it is. Will you fall on your face sometimes? Yes. Will critics take their shots and revel in your every misstep? Count on it. Tearing down, after all, is much easier than building up. But this commitment to excellence, this passion to get better, truly is the heart of a champion. It is what energizes everything we do at Ohio State. There is a red line at the edge of our practice field. Every day before practice, I stand at that red line and watch the guys take the field. The rule is that once they cross that red line, they are not only running—they are prepared to give all that they've got. If I don't like somebody's demeanor—it could be body language, a look on a guy's face, anything—I turn him around and point to the locker room. You better be ready to go; otherwise, don't come on the practice field.

How much do we value leadership at Ohio State? We have developed an in-depth, systematic approach to leadership training that we implement in our off-season. Tim Kight leads workshops with the entire coaching staff, and he does the same for our players. There are quizzes, skill-building exercises, and deep discussions about how the principles apply in real-life situations. It is highly focused and purposeful, and it has greatly enhanced the way we develop leaders and build the culture of our team. It has had a huge impact on our players' and coaches' performance.

Many coaches think that you can build leadership by hanging motivational posters in the weight room, putting quotes in the team room, showing inspirational videos, and bringing in occasional speakers to energize the team. But by themselves, those tactics don't work.

I've always taught leadership to my teams, but now we go about it more methodically. Leadership is a skill, and like all skills it takes time and effort to develop. The timeworn quotes that have been hanging around locker rooms for years are not nearly enough.

Now I understand. Average leaders have quotes. Good leaders have a plan. Exceptional leaders have a system.

||||||||||||||||||

Ashtabula is an old port city that is a Hail Mary pass from Lake Erie in the northeast corner of Ohio. It derives its name from a Native American word that means "always enough fish to be shared around," and once was a major stop on the Underground Railroad back in the day. Bob Dylan mentioned it in a song in the 1970s, but all I knew on that May afternoon in my senior year at St. John is that the city of Ashtabula was where I let my team down, and where I was going to do my penance by making the eight-mile run home. I took off from Cederquist Park and plodded up the hill on Lake Avenue, before I turned on to Carpenter Road and then made my way onto Lake Road, where I pounded out the final miles, the hulking lakefront factories belching smoke as I went. I was nobody's long-distance runner, then or now. When I finally arrived at the modest Meyer residence, I looked out toward the lake and then went in the backyard and hit baseballs off a batting tee for over an hour.

There may be people who hate losing more than I do, but I'm not sure where to look for them. When I played high school sports, I had a close friend named Greg (Mac) McCullough. We played in the defensive backfield together in football, and he was my double-play partner at second base in baseball, but Mac's best sport was basketball. Though he was a good four inches shorter than me, he had a deadly shot and a keen sense of the game. We used to play one-on-one to fifty. I'd dive for loose balls, throw elbows, draw charges. I'd come off the court bloodied and bruised, and so would he. You would've thought an NBA title was at stake, not backyard bragging rights by Lake Erie.

I grew up, but the losses never got much easier. If you had seen me after Ohio State's loss to Michigan State in the Big Ten championship game at the end of 2013, you would have no doubt about that. A photo that went viral after that game showed me sitting on a golf cart eating pizza in the concrete underbelly of Lucas Oil Stadium in Indianapolis. I do not look happy. I wasn't happy. It was the end of my second year at Ohio State, and we'd won twenty-four straight games, and our full expectation was that we'd be playing for a national championship. Instead we got drubbed, 34–24, a defeat that exposed weaknesses that I had tried to ignore but no longer could. The mood got no better after we lost the Orange Bowl to Clemson, a game in which we gave up 576 yards, and our defense looked as if it were playing two-hand touch.

As distraught as I was at the way the season ended, I can tell you now that it was the most productive pain I ever could have experienced. It forced me to reevaluate every aspect of what we were doing and to be brutally honest with myself. That kind of honesty, whether it's a hard look at yourself or your team, is not easy. It requires time, effort, and courage, and probably courage most of all. If you don't identify and expose the issue, you are never going to be able to solve it. If you try to ignore a problem, or run from it—whether it's poor punt coverage, an underperforming employee or department in your company, or a growing disconnect in your marriage—it is only going to get worse.

Honesty is one of our core values at Ohio State. Honesty and its first cousin, accountability, are the heart of what we do, and that goes for everybody, staff and players alike. If you avoid the truth as a coach, you are teaching your players that it's OK to do the same thing. If you don't hold yourself accountable for your decisions and your actions, why should your star quarterback or punter hold himself accountable? You cannot have a close, meaningful relationship in this world without honesty. In 2001, I was an assistant coach under Bob Davie at Notre Dame when I interviewed for, and was offered, the job at Bowling Green, which had just come off a 2–9 season. I badly wanted to be a head coach, but was this the place? I mean, look at the job I had in hand. I was an assistant at as prestigious a school as there is in the country—a position that would be coveted by about a million young coaches. Was I going to give that up to take over a struggling team in the Mid-American Conference? I was having some major reservations. I reached out to the man who hired me at Notre Dame, a great mentor to me, Lou Holtz.

"Coach, I don't know what I should do," I said. "This isn't a very good job."

"Of course it's not a good job," Holtz said. "If it was a good job, they certainly wouldn't be talking to you."

He had a point. An excellent one. You have to start somewhere. So I took the job, and it launched me on my way as a head coach. Lou Holtz's honesty saved me from doing something stupid.

Late in 2010, my final season at the University of Florida, our daughter Gigi was being celebrated at her high school with a ceremony to commemorate her signing a letter of intent to play Division I volleyball for Florida Gulf Coast University. Gigi was looking forward to being a collegiate athlete. I was in a different place. I had been so consumed with my job that I hadn't been taking care of myself physically, and it was beginning to take its toll. We'd won two national championships and had a great run at Florida, but I had lost my perspective and my priorities. I knew this ceremony meant everything to Gigi, but true to dysfunctional form, I decided that I was too busy with Florida football to attend.

When I told that to Nancy Scarborough, my administrative assistant, she got in my face and ordered me to go to the ceremony.

"I can't go," I said. "I have too much to do."

"You are going to that ceremony and you are going now," she said. "Now get out of here."

So I went. About a hundred people were gathered in the auditorium. Gigi was on stage, at a desk, ready to sign her letter. It was such a special moment for her. I felt so proud and excited about the next step she would be taking in her life. I was standing next to my wife, Shelley, who was positively aglow. Then it was time for Gigi to speak. She looked lovingly at her mother and thanked her for always being there, at every game and tournament, and for all the rides to practice, for listening and supporting her, for everything. Shelley did all the heavy lifting in those days. She deserved to be singled out, richly.

And then Gigi looked at me.

"Dad, even though you couldn't always be there, I love you and thank you," she said.

In typical form, I overreacted. I felt a spike through my heart. In my mind I had become that guy—the guy who was extremely successful but whose priorities were askew, who missed key events as his children were growing up. I had become the guy I never wanted to be.

Gigi had no intention of calling me out. She knew that I had always been a loving father. Nevertheless, it was devastating to hear, and I felt that I had let her down. As I drove back to the football facility, I began to reevaluate my priorities. I had to be honest with myself.

There was a lot of honesty that went around the Ohio State football office in the winter of 2014, after the back-to-back losses to Michigan State and Clemson. It started with a five-minute lowlight film of the season, put together by Mickey Marotti, my longtime strength and conditioning coach, and David Trichel, our video coordinator. They are two key guys in my football cabinet, and they outdid themselves with the film. It was a horror show all the way. No popcorn was served. It showed Michigan State and Clemson celebrating their victories over us. It showed missed tackles and blown assignments, fumbles we lost and passes we dropped. It was so brutal to watch that some of the players were crying. I left the room because I thought I might get physically sick. The upshot of it was a painstaking assessment of where we fell short, what we needed to fix, and ultimately, the hard work we needed to do to improve how we lead, how we bond, how we teach, and how we behave. Notice I didn't say anything about blocking or tackling, or special teams. I've come to learn that your football system gets better when your leadership system gets better.

Everything we did from that moment forward was done with an eye toward making ourselves better, every single one of us. We were good; 12–2 is a season a bunch of teams would love to have. But we wanted more. We wanted to be great, and we were ready to do everything we possibly could to find that greatness.

That process began with establishing our Clarity of Purpose, capital letters intended.

Defining that Clarity of Purpose, I believe, is the most important first step a leader can take, whether you are in charge of a high school or a global conglomerate or a football team. It is fundamentally a mission statement, stripped to its most basic level.

Think hard. Be as specific as possible. Ask yourself: "Exactly what is it that I am after every day?"

If you are Federal Express, your clarity of purpose is get it there. If you are Disney, it is make people happy. If you are the Ohio State football team, it is

Nine Units Strong.

Offensive line, tight ends, quarterbacks, running backs, receivers, defensive line, linebackers, cornerbacks, and safeties—those are the units we are talking about. We need them all to operate at maximum capacity. That is Nine Units Strong.

There can't be any holdouts if you want to achieve your purpose, no splinter groups with their own agendas, or the whole thing will implode. Purpose is what drives all that we do, the high-octane fuel that energizes us. Without it, you can work hard and do all sorts of things right and still not get the results you want. Think of an eight-man rowing team in the Olympics. Their goal is to get across the line first and win the gold. To achieve it, they have to row in perfect synchronization, all eight sets of oars moving water in unison; one rower who is out of sync or not doing his part will compromise everything.

When we lost those games at the end of the 2013 season, we were not operating at maximum capacity. We were three units short of being Nine Units Strong. And when you are competing against a team with equal talent, that will not get it done. The challenge, of course, is building a culture that enables you to perform at Nine Strong. It is leading in a way that aligns, empowers, and motivates your people. It is what we learned to do, week by week, in the 2014 season.

I've had the great fortune to coach some incredibly gifted and selfless players and win three college football championships in the last ten years. Do I have all the answers? I don't have half of them. But I'll tell you what: I am looking hard for the ones I don't have. During the year following my resignation from Florida, while working for ESPN, I went on a fact-finding mission. I took stock of myself and opened up to the possibility of change—not an easy thing for any of us to do. I sought insights from coaches and leaders I respect. I visited with Bob Stoops at Oklahoma, Mack Brown at Texas, and Chip Kelly, then at Oregon. I spent important time with Phil Knight, chairman and cofounder of Nike, a friend and mentor who has had a profound impact on my life.

I stayed up until 4 A.M. one night reading a remarkable book called *Lead . . . for God's Sake,* by Todd Gongwer, a parable about a coach who completely loses his way before embarking on a spiritual journey that reconnects him with the reasons he wanted to coach in the first place. Todd didn't know it, but he was writing the story of my life (so much so that I wrote the foreword for future editions of the book).

As I met with each leader, my greatest question was: How do you maintain work–life balance, especially in a sport like football, which demands so much of your time and attention? Near the end of my time in Florida, I had lost thirty-seven pounds and had chest pains and thought I was dying. One night I fell out of bed and sprawled facedown on the floor, my chest feeling as if it were being crushed by an anvil as Shelley, a trained nurse, spoke to a 9-1-1 operator. My friend Randy Walker, the coach at Northwestern and a man I had great admiration for, had died of a heart attack at age fifty-two just a few years before.

Was I going to be next?

My soul-searching trip also took me to West Point, accompanied by our son, Nate. We stayed at the house where the legendary Army coach, Red Blaik, used to live. I met with Rich Ellerson, then the Army coach, and we went to a little café not far from the West Point cemetery, near Blaik's gravesite. We drank coffee and talked about finding clarity and doing things for the right reason, not for money and glory and national championships. Rich invoked the West Point mission: "To educate, train and inspire." The trip gave me a lot to think about. I kept searching. I took another trip, this one with my daughters, Nicki and Gigi, starting with three days in Rome before we flew to Israel and retraced the steps of Jesus. As a devout Catholic, my faith is very important to me; to share this journey with my daughters meant everything. After watching Mel Gibson's

The Passion of the Christ in Rome the night before, we flew to Israel and went to Bethlehem and Nazareth and Capernaum, where Jesus started his ministry. We went to the River Jordan, where Jesus was baptized by John the Baptist, and we walked the *Via Dolorosa* (or Way of Suffering), the path Jesus followed in Old Jerusalem while carrying the cross on the way to his Crucifixion. In the Garden of Gethsemane, we saw where Jesus prayed the night before he was crucified and later touched the rock that his cross was laid against on the morning of the Resurrection.

The whole experience was deeply humbling. To witness the place where Jesus died for our sins, to be in the exact place where He rose from the dead, put everything in perspective. To share it with my daughters was unforgettable.

Now more than ever, I am committed to enjoying the journey of my life as a leader, coach, husband, and father. I think if you asked Shelley, Nicki, Gigi, and Nate, they'd tell you that now I'm more present and more devoted than I've ever been. I cringe when I look back at how I was at age thirty-six, when I got my first head coaching job at Bowling Green. I was a raving lunatic a lot of the time. It might've changed a bit at Utah and Florida, but not by much. These days I am much more purposeful and intentional. That doesn't mean I am not confrontational or that I don't have high expectations. If you took a survey of people at Woody Hayes Athletic Center, they would be sure to confirm that for you. But rather than just shredding somebody when something goes wrong, I am more inclined to take a step back and evaluate where things jumped the tracks and then seek to fix it.

My friend Tim Kight came into my life, providentially, after the 2012 season, and his leadership advice is an important part of the story of the 2014 season and beyond. Tim was recently asked by a reporter: "Since coming to Ohio State, how has Urban Meyer changed?" Here's what Tim said:

In the old days Urban got furious. Now, he gets curious. Yes, Urban is old school. He is very demanding and pushes hard. His standards are clear, and he expects that coaches and players perform to those standards. He will get in your face very fast if you are not doing your job. But Urban is also deeply committed to equipping his coaches and players with the skills and tools to do their job. The amount of training that he has done with his team—coaches and players—is unprecedented. Probably more than any team in college football history. He is constantly filling their tool box.

Urban believes the trust component is essential. He has learned in our training that you can only push people as far as the level of trust you have built with them. Pushing hard without trust doesn't work. Players today want a strong connection with their coaches. So Urban makes trust building a priority. A big priority.

Today's players also want to know what, how, and why. It's not enough to just say, "Do this and that." So Urban does a great job of communicating the why. That's what his emphasis on clarity of purpose is all about. It's not just the big purpose, it's also the purpose of so-called little things. Urban makes sure that everything that is done at OSU football has purpose. There is nothing accidental.

To summarize, I think that at more than any time in his coaching career, Urban focuses on the powerful combination of these elements: clarity of purpose + deep trust + high standards + consistent accountability + tools that empower. He fully understands that these things are what produce elite team performance.

Urban is no less demanding today than in years past, but he is more developmental. His message: "Here is the standard I demand. Here are the tools you will need in order to meet that standard. And by the way, I love you guys."

So rather than get angry when he doesn't get the results he wants, he looks to the system. At what point did it break down? Trust too low? Purpose unclear? Lack of skills? Low accountability? Player mismanaged his response?

Again, in the old days he got furious. Now, he gets curious."

I do know that I am much better at finding joy and being grateful for each day and for all the blessings God has bestowed upon me. To me, the essence of life and leadership is change and growth. It is about pushing yourself to improve every day in whatever you do. I truly believe in the maxim that if you are not getting better, then you are getting worse. Do you know many people who wake up in the morning and say, "Today, I am committed to being mediocre?" I don't. I believe most people want to give the best they have but don't have the necessary tools and mindset to get there. That's where leadership comes in. I go back to the way companies like Apple and Nike operate, and their willingness to continually push the envelope. It's exactly what we want our players at Ohio State to do. We push our players every day. We train, coach, and perform at the highest possible level. And that level is not for everyone. I often refer to our players as elite warriors, not because they are going to war and certainly not because what we are doing is anything remotely as serious as war, but because they are trained in an incredibly rigorous way and are constantly engaged in physical, mental, and spiritual combat.

Many of our players and coaches have experienced profound changes in their lives, on and off the field, by embracing the ideas you are about to read. I would encourage you to see whether these ideas can have the same result for you.

If you are responsible for leading people, your challenge is to bring them along with you, help them live and work and play with passion and achieve things they never thought possible. In the pages that follow I lay out the leadership template that made the journey of our 2014 championship season so rewarding. I hope you find it helpful.

||||||||||||||||||

Prologue: Above the Line Playbook

- Leadership isn't *a* difference maker. It is *the* difference maker.

- Leadership is much more than simply declaring what you want and then getting angry if you don't get it.

- A leader is someone who earns trust, sets a clear standard, and then equips and inspires people to meet that standard.

- Be true to who you are.

- Talk straight and demand accountability.

- Run toward problems. If you ignore them, they only get worse.

- Work to get better every day. Staying the same gets you nowhere.

- Savor the journey. Every day. You only get to do it once.

||||||||||||||||||

ONE

The Foundation

ABOVE THE LINE

L et's get something straight before we go any further: Ohio State won the 2014 national championship because we have great players who played great. The coaching staff can make a significant impact, but the athletes on the field are the ones who make the plays. It bothers me when I hear so-called experts going on and on about coaching brilliance and how somebody's schemes are so much better than everybody else's.

That's nonsense.

In my fourth game at Ohio State in 2012, we played the University of Alabama–Birmingham in Ohio Stadium. This is the same UAB team that would go 3–9 that season and later decide to discontinue its program (a move the school eventually reversed). We were pathetic. We played lethargically for much of the game, and the result was that a 37-point favorite was in a one-score game in the fourth quarter. Then our quarterback, Braxton Miller, took over on a late drive, passing for 35 yards, running for 26, and scoring the game-clinching touchdown and 2-point conversion. We didn't win that game because of superior schemes or Urban Meyer's genius. We beat UAB for one reason: Braxton is a big-time player, and his performance led our team to victory.

Where the coach's job comes in is to get great players to play great. That is the responsibility of any leader in any organization. And it is what the core of this book is about: leading and motivating people to perform at their best and to exceed what they thought possible. As I often remind our coaches and support staff, we are at Ohio State for one reason, and that is to make the student-athlete's experience as successful as it can be, equipping him with the tools and the work ethic that will enable him to compete and win in every aspect of his life.

Becoming a truly effective leader is a big challenge, and like everything else important in this world, it doesn't happen all at once. You don't wake up and say, "I'm going to run a marathon," and then take off for 26.2 miles. You train. You work diligently on building the fitness and mindset you need to achieve your goal. It's no different in the leadership realm. You don't just pull into the office one day and decide "I'm going to become a great leader today," and you definitely don't get it done by watching an inspirational video and finding some good quotes to put on the walls. You have to work at it and have an unyielding passion to get better every day.

It all begins with Above the Line behavior. It is a Tim Kight teaching point, and it has deeply influenced how I lead and how I think. I was blown away by its force and clarity when he first explained it to me, and, if anything, my appreciation for it has grown.

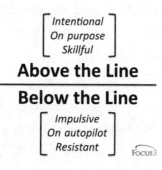

The performance of a team rises or falls on behavior. Winning behavior is intentional, on purpose, and skillful. It is Above the Line. But it's easier to be impulsive, on autopilot, and resistant. This is Below the Line. Below the Line is dangerous because it is comfortable and convenient. It is the path of least resistance. Below the Line takes little effort or skill, and the best it can produce is "just OK." Eventually, it produces failure.

The simple truth is that getting and staying Above the Line is the foundation of success in anything you do—work, school, football, and life. The harder truth is that getting and staying Above the Line is not easy. It must be taught and developed. Every day is a battle for whether we choose to live Above the Line or Below the Line. The choice we make determines how we treat the people we love, how we interact with colleagues at work, how we do our job, how we learn and grow, how we deal with adversity and disappointment, and ultimately what we achieve.

Please stop a moment and take this in: *Above the Line behavior is the foundation of success in anything you do.* There isn't an aspect of your life that is untouched by it, and because of that, the decision to behave Above the Line or Below the Line is the most important choice you make every day. Above the Line behavior is conscious and thoughtful—a choice made in alignment with your larger vision of where you want to go. Below the Line behavior is directed by impulse or the gravitational pull of old habits; you just react without thinking. Below the Line is your default response. It is my default response, too.

Somebody cuts you off in traffic. Your boss selects a co-worker for a promotion that you thought you deserved. Your spouse does something that irritates you. You have a choice to make. How are you going to respond?

You are a secondary coach and you see a referee throw a flag on the 1-yard line for pass interference, and you immediately have a meltdown, throwing up your arms and screaming at the guy, "That's terrible. He didn't even touch him!" (Even though you know he did.) Do you do this because it's smart? Productive? Because it's in your best interests? No. You do it because you're on autopilot, ruled by impulsiveness. Below the Line behavior is not only counterproductive, it completely sabotages your purpose.

Years ago I was a hothead during games, a guy who would rip into referees, chase them down the field, and throw and kick stuff along the way. I did that because I was immature and gave in to impulsive behavior. Never mind that it accomplished nothing, and set a terrible example for my team—basically telling them that it's OK to look for a scapegoat when things go wrong. I didn't think. I just reacted. Below the Line.

I used to send text messages during Mass, all the time. I tried to be discreet, but Shelley knew what I was doing and wasn't happy about it. I am a God-fearing Irish Catholic who has been going to church my whole life, yet in the height of my maniacal-pursuit-of-perfection days at Florida, here I was, transacting football business in a pew, tuning out the homily so I could suggest a new short-yardage play to our offensive coordinator, or tell a recruit's mother why she should entrust her son to me. I had convinced myself that if I wasn't on the job at all times, I was falling behind. That is classic, resistant, impulse-driven Below the Line behavior.

One time I chewed out an *Orlando Sentinel* reporter for misquoting a Florida receiver who implied that Tim Tebow was not "a real quarterback." I was ticked off that the reporter had used the receiver for a story and tried to make the receiver and Tebow look bad. But I handled the situation very poorly, and all it did was make things harder for everybody. I wound up apologizing to the guy, but by then the Below the Line damage had been done.

It isn't hard to find people who are caught up in Below the Line behavior. All you need to do is look for those whose first reaction is to *b*lame (others), *c*omplain (about circumstances), and *d*efend (yourself), or BCD. At Ohio State, BCD is the worst thing you can do, outside of lying or disrespecting a woman. It is much worse than fumbling or throwing an interception. When there is a lot of BCD going on, it means people are not owning their mistakes, not being accountable, and it typically means you are continually hearing variations of the following:

- *"No way could they have scored if the safety had supported me the way he was supposed to."*

- *"Coach has no clue what I can do. I've got to get out of here and go where I am appreciated."*

- *"It's not our fault we don't have the talent we need to be competitive. The previous staff did a terrible job of recruiting."*

- *"If I had a quarterback with a better touch on the ball, I'd be the best receiver in the nation."*

- *"You can't blame me for missing that block. They had a different short-yardage defense than the one we saw on film."*

And on and on it goes, in business, academia, politics, everywhere. My advice to leaders: ruthlessly eliminate BCD. Instead of accountability, BCD creates a culture of excuse making and victimization—things that are toxic for your organization and performance. It has never solved a problem, achieved a goal, or improved a relationship. Stop wasting your time and energy on something that will never help you.

You can find a thousand excuses in the game of football.

Some of them might even be legitimate, but we don't want to hear them at Ohio State. You screw up, you own it, and then you work twice as hard to make sure it doesn't happen again.

No BCD.

At Ohio State, we fight for Above the Line behavior in everything we do. Coaches, staff, players. Academics, football, social life. We understand the value of Above the Line. We also understand the cost of Below the Line.

In the winter and spring of 2014, we invested a great deal of time and effort training our team in Above the Line behavior. First we taught it to our assistant coaches (or as we call them, unit leaders), who in turn taught it to the players. The purpose was to embed Above the Line thinking and behavior into every facet of Ohio State football.

O ur collective ability to stay Above the Line in 2014 was put to the test even before the season started. Ten days prior to our first game, I was standing on the field during an afternoon practice, a couple of yards away from Braxton Miller, who was dropping back, looking to his left, about to throw a pass. Braxton had suffered a serious shoulder injury in the Clemson game to end the previous year, and though he'd worked diligently on his rehab, he still didn't seem all the way back. A lot of people figured he'd be in the hunt for the Heisman Trophy, and I thought he might be too, but for now we had to nurse him through the first few weeks until his shoulder got stronger.

Braxton stepped up and threw a 7-yard out, and the next sound I heard was a loud, piercing shriek of pain. It's the worst sound you can ever hear on a football field.

Braxton was on the ground, obviously hurting badly.

"It came out again," he said though gritted teeth. "I can't believe it. It's out again."

I leaned over him and touched him on the helmet. "It's OK, Brax. It's going to be OK," I said.

It wasn't OK. Braxton Miller was done for the year.

It meant that a team with massive question marks now had another one. A very big one. We had nine new starters on offense, including four on the offensive line. Among them was Braxton's replacement, redshirt freshman J. T. Barrett, who would soon become one of the few freshmen quarterbacks ever to start the season for OSU. On defense we had lost two truly great players, Ryan Shazier and Bradley Roby, to the NFL draft, both taken in the first round. On offense, two of our captains, Braxton and tight end Jeff Heuerman, were out with injuries.

We had a leadership void.

Usually there is great energy and excitement before you open a season. But given the challenges we were now facing, our confidence was low and our anxiety was high.

Our first game of the year was against the Naval Academy at M&T Bank Stadium in Baltimore, and for a good part of it you couldn't tell the Big Ten powerhouse from the service academy. Navy, a very good team coached by Ken Niumatalolo, runs a triple-option attack (the wishbone), and runs it extremely well. It is an offense that has been around since the earliest days of football, but we could not stop it. Navy shredded us so badly that we gave up more rushing yards (370) than we had in nearly twenty years. On offense, we had the ball inside Navy's 12-yard line three times in the first half and came away with a total of 3 points. Our young offensive line was struggling. Our quarterback, J. T. Barrett, was playing in his first game in two years after recuperating from a serious ACL (anterior cruciate ligament) tear. We were down by a point at halftime. We easily could've fallen into BCD mode.

But there was none of that.

In one corner, I saw Tom Herman, our quarterbacks coach, going over adjustments with J.T. Nearby, Ed Warinner, the offensive-line coach, was instructing his unit about ways to create holes in the Navy defense. On the other side of the room, Luke Fickell and Chris Ash, co–defensive coordinators, were making the necessary adjustments to slow Navy's option machine. I wasn't happy with how the opening half went—not at all. We just weren't a good team at that point. I knew we had good players, albeit inexperienced, but we weren't Nine Strong.

I knew that the worst thing I could do was panic. When you feel you've put the right people and the right program in place, you can't just blow it up in a fit of Below the Line frustration. Our players were going hard, they just weren't playing very well. I could see the benefits of all the work we'd done on staying Above the Line and it's critical as a leader to trust in your training. I liked what I was seeing everywhere but on the field, and I trusted that our level of play would elevate to the level of our training. Nobody was dishing blame or playing the victim;

the sole focus of everyone in that locker room was finding solutions.

We were in a street fight, and our whole goal as the day went on in M&T Bank Stadium was to find a way to win and get out of there. We did just that, finally getting a good lick on Navy's quarterback, forcing a fumble that linebacker Darron Lee returned 61 yards for a touchdown. Soon after, J.T. hooked up with Devin Smith on an 80-yard touchdown pass.

We wound up winning 34–17, and as we headed off the field, the best thing besides the victory was the unit togetherness we showed under adverse circumstances, and the fact that there wasn't any BCD.

We stayed Above the Line.

If you spent a season with us at Ohio State, you would hear me constantly talk about Above the Line behavior. That's because I know that if we all embrace it—coaches and players alike—we will be a team that has an uncommon commitment to each other and to the hard work necessary to achieve our mission. We will be a team that pushes relentlessly to train and perform at the highest level. And it starts with leadership. If you want the people on your team to perform Above the Line, then you must lead Above the Line.

During one of our early leadership sessions, Tim Kight drew a diagram on the board, with Above the Line behavior on top and Below the Line behavior on the bottom. He made it exceptionally clear that the best teams—the elite teams—are Above the Line in everything they do.

When Tim sat down, I walked up to the board. I looked at our players and I pounded my fist on the top of the diagram.

"This is what we are fighting for," I said. "This is what we are training for. This is where we want to be. Here. Right here. Always. Above the Line."

It was a hot morning in late August 2014, and Shelley and I were in the kitchen. It was the day after the Navy game. We were talking about the season's prospects overall. I said that with all the new players we had, and an untested quarterback, this season had a chance to be very much a rebuilding year.

"I really don't know about this team yet," I said. "Could it wind up being eight and four? Seven and five? It could. It's hard to say. I just think that with all our youth and inexperience, we may take some lumps before we reload in 2015." To me, this was being much more realistic than pessimistic. Still, there was something that intrigued me about the makeup of these guys. I left my home for the office at 5:30 the next morning, my usual time. It's my favorite time of day, the roads empty, dawn not yet even stirring, and the promise of a new day before me. I love what I do. I love the daily challenge of leading a team and building a culture.

I reflected again on how our team performed against Navy. Yes, we made mistakes. But I also saw our players, many of them starting for the first time, answer the stress of the Navy game with poise and maturity and Above the Line behavior. We weren't Nine Units Strong or even close to it, but I saw young men who sure looked as if they wanted to be Nine Strong.

I pulled into the Woody Hayes Athletic Center. It was still pitch black. I went to work.

Maybe they are going to fool me, I thought.

|||||||||||||||||||

Chapter One: The Foundation Playbook

- Every day is a battle for how you will live your life: Above the Line or Below the Line.

- Above the Line behavior is intentional, on purpose, and skillful. Below the Line behavior is impulsive, on autopilot, and resistant.

- Getting and staying Above the Line is the foundation for success in anything you do. It does not come naturally. It must be taught and learned.

- The best outcomes are the result of getting and staying Above the Line. The people and teams who consistently produce exceptional results are those who have trained themselves to perform intentionally, on purpose, and skillfully when it matters most.

- Beware of BCD: blame, complain, defend. BCD has never solved a problem, achieved a goal, or improved a relationship. Stop wasting your time and energy on something that will never help you. Ruthlessly eliminate BCD from your life.

- It starts with leadership. If you want the people on your team to perform Above the Line, then you must lead Above the Line.

|||||||||||||||||||

||||||||||||||||||||||||||||||||||||

TWO

The R Factor

IT'S NOT WHAT HAPPENS THAT MATTERS.

IT'S HOW YOU RESPOND.

I t's fourth-and-long and you are down by a point in the fourth quarter. You are on the road, and the whole stadium is rooting against you. How do you get and stay Above the Line? How do you fight off the forces that want to drag you Below the Line? How do you bring your best when it matters most? It begins with a simple powerful equation that affects everything we do.

$$E + R = O$$
Event + Response = Outcome

This equation teaches something very important about the way life works. We don't control the events in life, and we don't directly control the outcomes. But we always have control over how we choose to respond. How we respond means every-thing.

We call it the R Factor.

Life, like football, is a constant flow of events. When Ryan Shazier declared for the 2014 NFL draft (selected fifteenth overall by the Pittsburgh Steelers) after his junior season, that was a significant E. When Braxton ripped up his shoulder on that day in August, it was a sudden and awful E. When Gigi reminded me at her signing ceremony that I often wasn't there, that was a very challenging E for me as a father. It's important to understand that success is not determined by the situations you experience. Success is determined by how you choose to manage the R.

Every day you make R Factor decisions. You choose what actions you will take or not take in pursuit of your goals. You choose whether to give up or persevere through the inevitable obstacles you will experience. You choose how to interact with people at work and family at home. Every day you make deci-sions about how to respond. And how you respond makes all the difference.

It is the factor that determines the quality of your life.

We began our annual leadership training in February 2013, two months earlier than normal. It was apparent we had a lead-ership void with the departure of such players as John Simon, Zach Boren, and Etienne Sabino. Coach Mick and I had teach-ing points for our leadership council and showed a video that reinforced our message. We selected nineteen specific players for our council. These were key players for us who had to become leaders if we were to have a successful season. Later that spring, I was searching for a way to enhance our training when I met Tim Kight, founder of Focus 3, a leadership development firm, at a charity event. As Tim and I talked, I was struck by how his philosophies on leadership and culture were virtually identical to my own. And I was intrigued by the simplicity and power of the R Factor equation.

We began teaching R Factor skills that would help our players to respond Above the Line in any situation they might face—social, academic, football. Football is a tough, violent game. Pain isn't just common. In many cases, it's a constant. Our goal was very simple: to make our players' R stronger than any E they might encounter.

"When that happens," Tim Kight says, "then nothing—and no one—can stop you."

One of the reasons we immediately liked $E + R = O$ is because Coach Mick's strength and conditioning program is designed to put players into challenging mental and physical situations in order to train them how to respond with toughness. The R Factor enhanced what we were already doing. Coach Mick gives our players very difficult Es and then challenges them to respond Above the Line. His strength and conditioning program develops the ability of our players to manage the R in response to whatever they face on the football field.

There are six R Factor disciplines that we teach to our players.

R:1 Press Pause

We teach our players, in response to any situation they face, to press pause and ask: *What does this situation require of me?*

Pressing pause gives you time to think. It gets you off autopilot and helps you gain clarity about the outcome you are pursuing, the situation you are experiencing, and the Above the Line action you need to take to achieve the outcome.

There are two important benefits of pressing pause:

A) It helps you avoid doing something foolish or harmful.
B) It focuses you on acting with purpose to accomplish your goals.

A productive pause could last only a split second, which helps you regain your focus and take control of your action. It could last an hour, a day, or longer. The purpose is to take the time necessary to be intentional about the way you think and act. Pressing pause does not come naturally; it is a skill that must be developed. The more you practice, the more skilled you become at being able to identify how and when to use it effectively.

R:2 Get Your Mind Right

Elite performers win in their minds first. The mind is a battleground where the greatest struggle takes place. The thoughts that win the battle for your mind will direct your life. Mental state affects physical performance. The mind constantly sends messages to the body, and the body listens and responds. Therefore, elite warriors train their minds to focus and think in a way that maximizes how they practice and how they perform in competition.

Getting your mind right means managing two things:

A) What you focus on.
B) How you talk to yourself.

If you focus on negative things and talk to yourself in negative ways, that will put you into a negative mindset. Your performance will suffer. If you focus on productive things and talk to yourself in productive ways, that will put you into a productive mindset. Your performance will be enhanced. We teach our players to replace low-performance self-talk with high-performance self-talk. We tell our players, "The voice in your mind is a powerful force. Take ownership of that force."

There are three distinct mindsets that affect how our players train and practice. The first two are Below the Line, the third is Above the Line.

- Irritated mindset: Comes from negative focus that is born of laziness and is resistant to the productive discomfort that real growth requires. The self-talk sounds like: "Forget that drill! Why are we doing this stuff?!"

- Survival mindset: Comes from a desire to take the path of least resistance. It focuses on what's comfortable and convenient. It's not focused on getting better. The self-talk sounds like: "Man, this workout sucks. When will this be over? Just get through it."

- Purpose mindset: This is the Above the Line way of thinking that we look for, encourage, and reward. It embraces productive discomfort because it knows that discomfort is necessary in order to practice and perform at an elite level. It wants to compete. The self-talk of the purpose mindset is: "This drill makes me better. It makes our team better. Bring it on!"

R:3 Step Up

There is an Above the Line response to every situation you face. It is your responsibility to understand the situation, be clear about what is required of you, then respond Above the Line. This is what it means to *step up*.

Your R is most important when the E is most difficult. The more challenging the event and the more difficult the outcome, the more Above the Line you need to be. You will face challenging situations that require you to elevate your game. These are the times when you must call upon your deepest capabilities and courage to respond with purpose and skill. This is when your R Factor matters most. Simply stated, Big Es and Big Os require Big Rs.

Under pressure, we do not rise to the occasion. We rise or fall to the level of our training. When contact is made, it is too late to train and build skill. We must prepare and develop our R Factor capacity before we experience challenging situations. Under pressure, the R Factor habits that will be available to you are the ones you have purposefully built into your life. Build your R Factor capacity now because you will need it in the future.

One last point that is enormously important: how you *feel* is not always the best guide for what you should do. There are times you will feel a strong impulse or desire to do something Below the Line. When that happens, use the skills that we are teaching you: press pause and ask yourself, "What does this situation require of me?" Then get your mind right and step up. Act with intention, not impulse. Fight for the Above the Line response.

Every team faces some kind of adversity. Mediocre teams are destroyed by it. Good teams survive it. Great teams get better because of it.

The 2014 Ohio State Buckeyes were a resilient football team. We faced adversity and got better because of it. But please understand: we were trained. No matter what we faced, we continually reminded our guys throughout the season as we were preparing for games, "You've been trained for this moment."

Resilience is one of life's most important attributes. Because nobody wants hardship or adversity, but everybody gets it. It's inevitable. No one escapes pain, fear, or difficulty. In fact, a productive and successful life involves some amount of necessary pain.

When it happens, don't run from it.

Learn from it.

B efore I move on to the final three disciplines, I would like to show you how valuable—even life-changing—R Factor training can be. A few days after we lost to Clemson in the Orange Bowl early in 2014, I was on the road recruiting in Florida. We were getting torn apart for our performance, especially for allowing their offense to pile up 497 yards, six touchdowns, and 40 points on our defense. People were calling for a major shakeup in our staff. It was the time of year when programs make changes. I have to admit, I was considering a couple of moves, and I had been contacted by some big name defensive coaches. What I needed to be clear about was that any change would be motivated by the right reasons. Reacting to shrieking callers on sports radio is not the right reason. Making our program better *is* the right reason.

I was sifting through all of this as I drove on Interstate 95, just north of Fort Lauderdale. I saw a rest stop and decided to pull over. My head was spinning. I do not take firing anybody lightly. I know that football is a bottom-line business—what business isn't?—but you are talking about people's livelihoods here. You are talking about good people, consummate professionals who care about doing a good job.

I did not want to screw this up.

I sat behind the wheel of my rental car, pressed pause, and prayed for clarity in the decision-making process. I thought about the counsel I'd received years earlier from Father James Riehle, a priest Shelley and I were very close to in my six years at Notre Dame. (He baptized our son, Nate.) After I got the Bowling Green job, Father Riehle and I met for coffee. He congratulated me on getting my first head coaching position. "I want you to keep something in mind," he said. "For your whole career as a coach you've been making suggestions. Now you are making decisions. Some of those decisions will have a great impact on people's lives. I pray that you will remember that and be very careful and prayerful when you make those decisions."

Cars zoomed past me on the interstate. I didn't want to be ruled by impulse or an urge to make a change just for the sake of change. I thought again about the men involved, their commitment to their work, and their character. Fifteen minutes later, I pulled back into traffic and continued on my way.

There would be no dismissals. It was the right decision all the way.

Before our 2015 season, one of our players was in a deep state of distress. It was about three o'clock in the morning. He'd just found out his girlfriend was cheating on him. They had an extremely heated argument, and his anger was rising. He could tell that he was on the brink of losing control and lashing out physically. He was close to doing something terrible that could change the course of his life, and it was at that exact point that he pressed pause and called his position coach. The coach picked up right away and could hear the depth of the player's hurt and anger. The coach talked to him, calmed him down, and helped him step back from the torrent of emotions and get his mind right. This player is a great young man who wants to do the right thing. He's not one of those players whom you are getting calls about every other day. He has made great decisions and been a model student-athlete ever since he stepped on campus. He made another great decision in this case by calling his coach. Would the outcome have been different if he hadn't managed his R and gone through all that Above the Line training? Would he have been able to press pause the way he did?

Or would his anger have gotten the better of him?

I'm quite sure I know the answers to these questions. It was an important and humbling reminder that living Above the Line can have an impact on matters far more important than the outcome of a football game.

R:4 Adjust and Adapt

The ability to be flexible and responsive in today's competitive environment is a mandatory skill. The best athletes and teams are exceptional at adjusting and adapting to changing circumstances. It is foolish to resent or resist change. A rapidly changing world deals ruthlessly with people who fail to adapt. If you don't like change, you are going to like irrelevance even less.

It is an inescapable reality—things change.

Here's another reality—life will get increasingly difficult for you if you don't.

Every day you are creating or reinforcing habits in your life. The question is, are they habits that help or habits that hold you back? Be quick to break the habits that will break you. Consider the current path of your R Factor habits and patterns. Where are they taking you? Decide whether that is where you want to go and whether you need to make adjustments.

If what you are doing isn't working, change it. Don't blame the E, choose a better R. Don't hold on to what's holding you back. Get rid of anything that does not make you better.

Make sure the habits you have today are in alignment with the dreams and goals you have for tomorrow.

R:5 Make a Difference

Your R is an E for others. Your attitude and behavior have a profound impact on your teammates and your coaches. The quality of your relationships is determined by how you choose to manage the R. You don't get the team you want—you get the team you build.

What kind of Es are you giving to your teammates and coaches? Make a Difference means taking complete ownership of the experience you give to teammates and the contribution you make to the culture of the team. The way you manage your R matters not just to you, but to the guys around you. The experience you give to others may be the single most important element of teamwork. You will be no better as a team than you are to each other. Make the people around you better.

R:6 Build Skill

At the level we compete, everyone has talent. Elite performers are the ones who are relentless about building skill beyond their talent. Talent is a gift. Greatness is a choice.

Talent can take you to a level of ability that produces good results. But talent by itself will not take you to the elite level. Exceptional performance is the result of an uncommon level of focus and discipline in the pursuit of greatness. Build skill every day and consistently get better. Be coachable. Train and practice Above the Line. Be intentional and on purpose. Complacency is the enemy of exceptional. Grow beyond your talent!

Embrace discomfort. Discomfort marks the place where the old way meets the new way. Discomfort indicates that change is about to happen. Push through the pain. If it doesn't challenge you, it will not change you.

The more you use these tools and develop your ability to manage the R, the more proficient you will become. The challenge is to consistently manage your R Above the Line.

That is the source of great Outcomes. That is the source of success in every dimension of life. Talent is a ticket that gets you into the game, but it's the ability to respond when it matters most that wins. We call it "reaches and reps." You reach a new level—an elite level—by continually pushing yourself through specifically designed repetitions, and doing it with uncommon dedication. We showed our team a video of Stephen Curry practicing, in which he displayed this kind of Above the Line training. It wasn't just that Curry took five hundred more shots a day than anybody else to become the NBA's Most Valuable Player, and to help bring an NBA championship to his Golden State Warriors for the first time in forty years. It was how purposefully he took those shots, how the specific techniques, whether shooting a jumper off a left-hand dribble or making a step-back three-pointer, would sharpen his skills so that in the heat of a playoff battle he would be masterful.

Champions are made by how they manage their R. Whatever other attributes they might have going for them, their ability to consistently respond to daily challenges with Above the Line behavior makes all the difference, just as the inability to respond in this way can cause significant problems. I've had experience with that, too. At the end of my time in Florida, I can see now that my Below the Line response to the Es that happened were the precise reason my Os were so poor. Minutes after we won our second national championship with a 34–24 triumph over Oklahoma early in 2009, you know what I did? I went into an office, closed the door, and started e-mailing recruits. All around me there was confetti flying and people celebrating, and I was locked away by myself, trying to get more players. A member of my staff knocked on the door and came in.

"What are you doing?" he said. "We just won the national championship. Let's go enjoy it!"

"I've just got to get a few e-mails out and I'll be out," I said.

I never made it out.

I was at the pinnacle of my profession and I was obsessed with what's next. For one thing, I'd been having chest pains of varying severity for three years—a terrifying thing to deal with because I naturally figured it was heart-related; only later did I find out that it was an esophageal spasm that mimicked heart pain. Beyond that, I'd become consumed not with teaching and leading and motivating, but with an obsessive pursuit of perfection. I was paranoid that somehow somebody was going to crack the code of what we had going at Florida, and that would be the beginning of the end. Nothing was going to be enough, and nothing would ever be enough, the way I was going. At the Southeastern Conference Media Day before the start of the 2009 season, a reporter asked me, "How does it feel knowing that anything other than an undefeated season and a national championship and you are a failure?"

Of course it's absurd to pronounce any season that isn't perfect a failure, and yet that was exactly my mindset; the fear of failing had blown right past the joy of winning. Think about that. You have something you are completely passionate about, something you've loved for almost as long as you've been alive, and something you are good at. Suddenly you find no joy or nourishment in it at all.

It was a sad state to be in.

The day after every win, we have what's called Victory Meal. It's a tradition I started at every school where I've been the head coach. The idea is to have a really nice postgame meal where the players can go and have fun and the coaches can relax and enjoy themselves, too. After a while I started missing an occasional Victory Meal, and then I began missing more. I had convinced myself that the work I had to do was more important than enjoying the moment and connecting with our players and staff. One time, after a victory over Georgia, I decided to make the Victory Meal for a change, and there was practically nobody there.

"Where is everyone?" I asked Coach Mick.

"They don't do it anymore because you aren't here," he said.

In the face of the event I was confronted with at Florida in 2009—the expectation of perfection—my response was awful. Consequently, the outcome was a lot of emotionally beaten up people and a painful loss in the SEC title game. This was the monster I had created. It was all mine.

I am a spiritual person, though I do not talk about it publicly that much. I read the Bible and pray, and like to begin the day texting a line or two of Scripture to the people I love. I believe that God has a plan for all of us. I did not know what the plan was at the end of my six years in Florida, but I did know that I badly needed to get my mind right and my priorities reordered, even if I wouldn't have used that vocabulary at the time.

I came across a book called *Change or Die*, by Alan Deutschman. It's primarily a how-to book for business leaders, and on page 150, there is a passage that reads:

"Why do people persist in their self-destructive behavior, ignoring the blatant fact that what they've been doing for many years hasn't solved their problems? They think that they need to do it even more fervently or frequently, as if they were doing the right thing but simply had to try even harder."

The author might as well have put my picture next to that statement. He was writing about me, even though I didn't see it. I began to gain insight into what I needed to change my life. How could I lead my players if I couldn't lead me? I was committed to finding a new way, a healthier and more balanced way. I've found it. It turned out to be the most productive discomfort I ever could have had.

I had a totally different sort of discomfort two games into our 2014 season. We returned home to Ohio Stadium after the scare against Navy, played a prime-time game before more than 107,000 fans, and got beaten by two touchdowns by a very talented but unranked Virginia Tech team. It was not only our first regular-season loss in my three years, it was our third loss in the last four games. That's an awful winning percentage (.250), and what made it worse is that we got completely outcoached.

And that is exactly what I told the media and everybody else right after the game.

We lost this game because of me. Because we weren't prepared. You want to bring the heat, bring it right here.

Virginia Tech has a defensive coordinator, Bud Foster, who has been with head coach Frank Beamer for nearly thirty years, and has a well-earned reputation as a creative defensive mind, a guy who devises fresh ways to confuse you and come after you almost every week. They had so much success blitzing us that J.T. completed only nine passes in twenty-nine attempts. They played a defensive scheme they had never shown before, and with our four new offensive linemen, we had trouble adjusting because we hadn't prepared them well enough.

We have a saying that is fundamental to what we do:

I see better than I hear.

Or as Andrew Luck told me, "Your actions are so loud I can't hear what you are saying."

Sometimes we express it another way: Don't give me theory. Give me testimony.

We are not measured by our intentions, but by our actions.

When you are a leader, your followers are watching everything you do. If your aim is to instill a culture of accountability and to model Above the Line behavior, you better have the courage to take the bullet when it is called for. Some leaders have a hard time with this. It's never been an issue for me. I can thank my father for that. Every day of my life, it was drilled into me: Do your work. Tell the truth. Own your mistakes. Respect your elders. Keep your mouth shut and do the right things. Never quit. Excuses, to my father, were the pathetic path of a weak man.

Quitting? That was even worse.

A few weeks into my minor-league baseball career in 1982, I was having a rough go of it down in Bradenton, Florida. I wasn't hitting, and I felt completely out of my element. Then, at shortstop one day, a bad-hop grounder smashed into my face, fracturing a bone near my eye socket. My eye was swollen shut for almost a week. The whole side of my face hurt. I thought it over and decided this pro baseball idea had been a mistake. I felt overwhelmed emotionally. I called home and told my father about the injury.

"I'm getting screwed, Dad. The manager can't even pronounce my name correctly. I'm not getting that much playing time. I think it's time to forget it and go to college," I said.

There was a momentary silence on the line. A very momentary silence.

"You can quit if you want," my father said. "You are a man now. Just know you won't be welcome in this house anymore. Call your mother on holidays."

Click.

I didn't quit.

Adversity afflicts all of us at some point, and I believe what I did after the Virginia Tech game is the most effective course of action for a leader. Go right at it, as hard as you can. Size up the situation and deal with it. It is what I knew I had to do two games into the 2014 season. I wasn't going to let the loss to Virginia Tech skew my thinking, no matter how disappointing it was and no matter how much of a hammering we were taking in the media because we'd lost a game we weren't supposed to lose. Afterward, the *Columbus Dispatch* said, "All the brave talk about how Ohio State would withstand the season-ending injury to Braxton Miller was just dead air. These Buckeyes are a rudderless ship on offense, and the defense isn't much better." The paper also said that we were "way, way, way overrated."

I had complete faith in what we were doing and how we were progressing. Our players and coaches were still confident. The units weren't perfect, but our players were working hard and getting better every day.

Our focus was highly targeted and our purpose was exceptionally clear.

Our season was far from over.

ııııııııııııııı

Chapter Two: The R Factor Playbook

- $E + R = O$

- Event + Response = Outcome

- Success is not determined by the situations you experience. Success is determined by how you manage the R.

- The R Factor disciplines are the essential skills for getting and staying Above the Line.

- There are six disciplines:

  - R:1 Press pause
  - R:2 Get your mind right
  - R:3 Step up
  - R:4 Adjust and adapt
  - R:5 Make a difference
  - R:6 Build skill

- Embrace productive discomfort. Discomfort marks the place where the old way meets the new way. Push through the pain. If it doesn't challenge you, it will not change you.

ııııııııııııııı

THREE

||||||||||||||||||||||||||||||||||||||

Creating a Culture

**LEADERS CREATE CULTURE. CULTURE DRIVES
BEHAVIOR. BEHAVIOR PRODUCES RESULTS.**

Not once in the 2014 season did I stand before the team and state that our goal was to win the national championship. It may seem counterintuitive, but it's the truth. Did we want to win a national championship? Absolutely. But it was not part of our daily discourse, ever. Our focus was entirely on Nine Units Strong and building a culture that motivated our players to train and compete at an elite level.

Culture is what we believe, how we behave, and the experience that our behavior produces for each other. That last point is critical. People experience culture through behavior. Strategy determines scheme and technique. Culture determines attitude and effort. Once strategy has been developed, success becomes a matter of attitude and effort. And that's where culture comes in.

Every team and every unit has a culture, either by design or by default. In order to get a culture by design, the behavior of everyone in the unit must be Above the Line. The way you respond creates the culture. This means you must respond with intention, purpose, and skill.

On a team driven by an intentional culture, attitude and effort are focused in the same direction, and the foundation for success has been created. Players have an uncommon commitment to each other and to the core beliefs of the team. Trust is strong. Units are aligned. Communication is real. Problems are solved. Effort is relentless and execution is exceptional. This is culture by design.

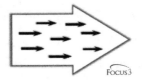

On a team with a less-than-effective culture, players and coaches are not in alignment. Trust is weak. Communication and teamwork are poor. There is a lot of BCD. Problems do not get resolved. Players hesitate to commit. Selfishness dominates. Attitude and effort are substandard. Accountability is inconsistent. This is culture by default.

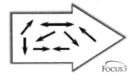

Your team, business, or organization will perform to the level of leadership you provide. It is no secret that the critical factor in the success of a business is the quality of its leaders. Remember, leadership isn't a difference maker, it is *the* difference maker. Often what differentiates a great business from an average business is the effectiveness of its leaders.

P erformance cannot be declared. It must be led. Great results are initiated and sustained by great leadership. Not just leaders at the top, but leaders at every level. Leadership is the triggering factor in the Performance Pathway.

LEADERS CREATE CULTURE. CULTURE DRIVES BEHAVIOR.
BEHAVIOR PRODUCES RESULTS.

Tim Kight introduced the Performance Pathway to me in the spring of 2013, and I immediately recognized its implications for our football team. These were things that I already believed, but Tim provided a crystal clear picture of the three critical elements we needed to focus on in order to produce exceptional results: leadership, culture, and Above the Line behavior.

In the winter of 2014, I asked Tim to teach the Performance

Pathway to our unit leaders. Our message was clear: the performance of the players in your unit is a reflection of the culture you create. It is your responsibility to create and build an Above the Line culture with your group. Notice the reinforcement loop between culture and behavior. This is the flywheel effect. Behavior reinforces the culture that creates it. Over time this mutual reinforcement gains momentum and becomes increasingly difficult to change. If you have the culture/behavior that you want, the flywheel effect works for you. If you do not have the culture/behavior that you want, the flywheel effect works against you.

Ironically, some coaches are so preoccupied with pushing for results that they fail to build a culture that sustains the behavior that produces results. But winning behavior will not thrive in a culture that does not support it.

As a leader, *you* are responsible for creating a winning culture that drives behavior and produces winning results. It's not someone else's job. It's your job!

Exceptional leaders create a culture that engages hearts and minds, energizes action, and executes with discipline. When that happens, the numbers and wins follow.

Culture eats strategy for lunch. Talent, schemes, tactics, and plans cannot replace a strong culture. A great culture can make even a mediocre strategy successful, but a weak culture will undermine even the best strategy. The foundation of culture is core beliefs. Not platitudes or quotes. Core beliefs. The beliefs that are the heart of the team.

There is a profound difference between a concept in your

head and a belief on your heart. When a belief is truly core, when it is fully and completely on your heart, then it will drive everything you do. You will respond in alignment with that belief no matter the event or situation. But if it is simply a concept in your head, if it is just a quote you find inspiring, then it will not consistently drive your actions. Especially not in response to difficult, challenging situations. Culture is what leads when no one is watching.

As part of our leadership training in the winter of 2014, we created a blueprint to communicate our culture to everyone on the team. The goal was to be so clear about our culture that there would be no confusion, no uncertainty, and no excuses. As you can see in the diagram below, our culture blueprint was designed to communicate three things: what we believe, how we behave, and the outcome we would achieve based on that

OSU FOOTBALL CULTURE BLUEPRINT		
What We Believe	**How We Behave**	**Outcome We Achieve**
Relentless Effort	Go as hard as you can, four to six seconds, point A to point B	We are tougher than any situation or opponent we face
Competitive Excellence	Constant focus on mental reps and game reps	You are prepared to make the play when your number is called
Power of the Unit	Uncommon commitment to each other and to the work necessary to achieve our purpose	Brotherhood of trust. Combat motivation.

belief and behavior. We communicated the culture blueprint with exceptional clarity and nonstop consistency to our team. And we held everyone accountable to it.

Our first core belief is relentless effort, and it means going as hard as you can. On every play. In every rep. All the time. The way we communicate it to our players is "Go as hard as you can four to six seconds from point A to point B." Notice the two components. There is the duration component—four to six seconds—because that's the length of the average football play, and there is the direction component—Point A to Point B—because in every drill and every play, our players have a designated start point and a specific end point. If you observe one of our practices, you will repeatedly hear guys shouting, "Four to six, A to B!" That is the sound of our coaches and players challenging guys to give relentless effort. It is nonnegotiable. Great effort can overcome poor execution, but great execution will not overcome poor effort.

The outcome we achieve by giving relentless effort is that we are tougher than any situation or opponent we face. At Ohio State, we believe that being elite is not about how talented you are, it's about how tough you are. Too often, coaches overemphasize avoiding mistakes, and as a result they paralyze the performance of their players. We acknowledge up front that mistakes are going to happen. I can handle a player making a mistake as long as he is going four to six, A to B, because a mistake is something we can and will fix. But a player who is lazy and gives partial effort will never perform at the standard that our game demands. This applies to the way my staff works as well. Clearly our coaches are not taking the snaps, but they are expected to work as hard as they can, getting from the point A of a task to point B so they can finish and move on to the next assignment. When it comes to the development of a team and a culture, I am relentless about relentless effort.

One of the best compliments I ever received was from the great John Robinson, former coach of UNLV and the Los Angeles Rams. After our Utah team beat UNLV, we shook hands at midfield and Robinson said, "Urban, that's the fastest team I've ever seen." Were we truly the fastest team ever to step foot on a football field? I'm sure we weren't. We had only a few players who ran a 4.5-second 40-yard dash or better, but that's how it looks when every player is going four to six, A to B.

Our second core belief is competitive excellence, and it means a constant focus on mental reps and game reps. It is the mindset of a winner. It is consistent engagement in your training and preparation. It is the mental makeup of a champion, the way elite competitors prepare. Competitive excellence is putting in the work necessary to remove all doubt in your ability to win your individual battle. We believe in two types of repetitions: game reps and mental reps. Game reps are performed during practice at game speed. I want to see guys compete. I want to know who can handle the pressure and rise to the maximum level of his training to win the game. Mental reps, on the other hand, are when you simulate those scenarios in your mind. Mental reps require no physical contact. Our players pay careful attention during practice and they make a detailed mental run-through of the play, executing slight movements with the correct steps and motions so that when they find themselves in game situations, they have correctly performed it both physically and mentally. Because football is so physically demanding, there are limited opportunities to practice at game speed and preserve our players' bodies throughout the season, making mental reps an essential part of our preparation. The outcome is that you are prepared to make the play when your number is called.

There is no better example than Kenny Guiton.

In 2012, Kenny was a junior backup to quarterback Braxton Miller. Throughout all of our practices that fall, Kenny was the most mentally and physically engaged player on our team. When Braxton was running plays, Kenny was 10 yards directly behind him, making the same reads and checks, executing the play mentally. Then, when the ball was snapped to Braxton, Kenny would perform the correct motions just as if he were taking the live rep. That was our culture at work. He was preparing in case his number would be called.

That October, Kenny's number was called. We were down against Purdue by 8 points. On the last play of the third quarter, Braxton went down and was injured for the rest of the game. Kenny came in. Two of his first three series did not end well, one with a safety and the other with an interception. It was the final drive of the game and we were down by 8 points with 60 yards to go, forty seconds left on the clock, and had no timeouts left. He led the offense down the field, and threw the game-tying touchdown pass to receiver Chris Fields with only three seconds left in regulation. On the very next play, Kenny tied the score on a perfectly executed pass play to tight end Jeff Heuerman for the 2-point conversion. After taking the game into overtime, running back Carlos Hyde dived over the line for the game-winning score.

We won that game and kept our undefeated season intact because Kenny Guiton fully embraced our culture of competitive excellence.

Our third core belief is power of the unit, and it means that our players have an uncommon commitment to each other and to the work necessary to achieve our purpose. Our team is organized into nine units. It is the responsibility of the unit leader to win the hearts and minds of the players in his group to create an unbreakable bond with and among his players. It is the responsibility of the unit leader to get each of his players to fully commit and take ownership of his contribution to the culture and performance of the team. The outcome we achieve is the brotherhood of trust and combat motivation. Our guys are motivated to play because of their love for each other and their love for their coaches.

The 2014 football team was one of the closest groups of players and coaches I've ever been around. It truly was a brotherhood. That didn't happen on its own, and it wasn't an accident. It was intentional. As I will explain later in this book, our coaches and players invested a great deal of time building their relationships with each other.

These are our core beliefs: relentless effort, competitive excellence, power of the unit.

This is our culture.

This is how we became Nine Units Strong.

B uilding a culture is a three-part process.

Believe it.

Sell it.

Demand it.

Believe It

First, you have to think deeply about the guiding principles and core values that you want at the heart of your organization. What behaviors are essential to execute your strategy, and what beliefs are essential to drive those behaviors? Identify the behaviors that are necessary to execute your strategy. Identify the beliefs that are necessary to drive and sustain those behaviors.

Second, examine yourself. Be honest and courageous. Do *you* believe in those core values and does your behavior reflect that belief? This is a critical question because your behavior sets the tone for the culture. The most important culture message you send is the way you behave. If it's not happening *in* you, it will never happen *through* you. If you don't believe it, no one else will believe it.

Sell It

Once your culture is clearly defined, communicate it to your players and staff with clarity and consistency, explaining why it is essential to the success of the program. This is not a debate. This is you as the leader standing before your team and building the foundation necessary for success. Your culture message must be exceptionally clear: no confusion, no uncertainty, no excuses. Explain to your team that this is what we believe and how we behave in all circumstances. It is who we are.

In 2014, once we defined the culture blueprint with exceptional clarity, we communicated it to the team. "This is the plan. The plan is infallible. Follow the plan."

Demand It.

When you determine what the culture is and communicate it with exceptional clarity, it is imperative that you hold people accountable to it. Let people know that adherence to the culture isn't merely an expectation, it is a requirement. The culture is the only acceptable standard of performance. One of the biggest mistakes leaders make is failing to hold people accountable for behavior that is inconsistent with the culture. Remember this: if you permit it, you promote it. It is essential that you challenge Below the Line behavior. It is also important to recognize and reinforce Above the Line behavior.

The leadership challenge is to build a culture that generates and sustains winning behavior. If you attack behavior without building the culture, the behavior may change temporarily, but it will eventually (probably quickly) revert. As I said earlier in this chapter, Above the Line behavior cannot thrive in a culture that does not support it. Make your cultural standards clear, hold people accountable to those standards, and the results will follow.

You don't get the culture you want; you get the culture you build.

If you are a leader who has been brought in to take over a program, before you even start building the culture, you need to do one very important thing: show respect and move on. Too often, when coming in to a new program or organization, people make the mistake of criticizing, directly or indirectly, the previous regime. Whatever business you are in, do not disparage your predecessors. Aside from being the wrong thing to do, there's no gain in it. You want everything to be about moving forward. Whoever you just took over for will still have constituencies within the organization and will not appreciate your criticisms, compromising your ability to influence and lead.

You've been hired to do a job, and that job is to lead

and coach—not to assess or dissect your predecessor's short-comings.

At every place I've coached, I've taken over for a man who was a good coach and highly regarded. At Bowling Green, I replaced Gary Blackney, who led the school to its first bowl victory and went 36–8–2 in his first four years. At Utah, I took over for Ron McBride, a superb coach who had the second most wins in school history and led Utah to a bowl-game victory over USC. At Florida I followed Ron Zook, also a very good coach, who had three winning seasons. And then came Ohio State, where I took over for interim head coach Luke Fickell, who had recently filled the position for Jim Tressel, whose ten-year record included six Big Ten titles, a national championship, and the first team ever to go 14–0 in a season.

It will be a long time before I forget my first meeting with the team after I had officially been introduced as the new coach. It was near the end of a year that had been devastating to all involved. The Buckeyes finished 2011 with only their sixth losing season since World War II. In the wake of the program's improper benefits investigation and Tressel's departure, Luke Fickell, a former Ohio State nose guard, a longtime assistant under Tressel, and an excellent football coach, took over on an interim basis on May 30, 2011. With so little preparation time before the season, it was a very difficult situation to say the least, not just because of the NCAA sanctions, but because a number of key players were implicated in the scandal and missed games due to suspensions. The team compiled a reasonable 6–3 record but struggled at the end of the regular season, losing its last three games by a total of 15 points. Ohio State was 6–6 going into a Gator Bowl showdown against my former program, Florida. With Luke's permission, I addressed the team in the team meeting room as they were preparing for the bowl game.

I stood before a team that looked defeated. The NCAA investigation, the suspensions, and the losses had taken an obvious toll on these young men. Slouched in their chairs, many with hoods on, this was a team that was clearly despondent.

"Sit up straight in your chair. Everybody! Now!" I said. "Take your hoods off right now. Show some respect!" My first impression of my future players was not positive, and it got even worse when I called my first meeting as coach after the bowl game loss. Five guys didn't bother to show up. We tried it again the next day. Several guys straggled in late.

I know how dispirited these guys were. Three weeks after I was hired, I got a call from athletic director Gene Smith telling me that the NCAA had hit us with another penalty—we weren't eligible to compete for a Big Ten title, bowl game, or the national championship. I felt robbed, and felt even more robbed on behalf of our players, but I also knew there was no sense playing the role of victim, or complaining to Gene, one of the greatest bosses I've ever had, or criticizing the NCAA in the media. I needed to stay Above the Line. All I could do was channel my efforts toward things that I could change. One of the first things I did was talk to all of our recruits and encourage them to stick with us because Ohio State was going to be back, and soon. I understood the recruits would be disappointed that they wouldn't be able to play in a bowl game as freshmen, and I knew rival schools would use the ban to lure them away from us.

I turned to what I knew would be the most challenging task of all: building a new culture. Morale was low, uncertainty was high, and all the stresses that afflict a college football operation when there is a staff change were very tangible. I knew there would be players, probably a good number of them and rightfully so, who had a deep connection with Coach Tressel and likely resented that I was here in the first place. As much empathy as I had for these players who were going through this upheaval, I could not let it deter me from what needed to be done. There was an attitude of negativity and distrust, and the time for change had arrived.

That change began the morning after the meeting when a number of players came in late.

At 4:55 A.M. Outside. In January.

This treatment lasted for the rest of the week. Day 1, as I recall, it was about thirty degrees with freezing rain, and it got worse as the week went on. The field was a slushy, icy mess. We kept them out there for ninety minutes. They had to do 400 yards of bear crawls, on all fours, going the length of the field four times. It was a miserable experience for all, but it had to be. I wanted to find out quickly who was in and who was out. Who were the guys I could count on to gut it out through terrible conditions and keep going? Who were the guys I could learn to trust? Zach Boren was one of the leaders on that team, a tough-minded fullback who had an older brother who played at Ohio State before him, and has a younger brother on the team now. Zach had been one of Coach Tressel's most loyal guys. Occasionally, he would wear a sweater vest—Tressel's signature wardrobe item—to remind everybody. I didn't mind. I have great regard for Jim Tressel. He was a great coach and a friend. But I had a culture to build, and I had to start immediately.

"This isn't a dictatorship," I told them. "You have your freedom. You don't have to stay. The door is right over there. But if you do stay and you want to be an Ohio State football player, you are not going to do it your way. You are going to do it our way."

My message from the beginning was simple and straightforward:

You did not choose me, I chose you. I am from Ohio. I have followed the Buckeyes since I was very young. I am moving my family here because I believe in Ohio State. With this privilege comes an incredible amount of responsibility and obligation. We have a plan and this plan works. The plan is guaranteed to work if every one of us is committed to it.

Just to make sure my point got across, I didn't even let the guys wear their OSU practice gear in the beginning. The shirts had to be worn inside out. They had to earn the right to wear them in the conventional way. They also weren't allowed in the locker room and had to change in their cars. It, too, was something they would have to earn. I wasn't optimistic that they would be in there any time soon.

The point of everything wasn't just to punish the guys for a careless attitude in our first two meetings. It was to jolt them out of their stagnation, and to show them (not tell them—a critical distinction) that if they weren't tough and weren't ready to push themselves beyond what they thought they were capable of, they might as well save us all the time and trouble and hand in their gear now.

On day 5, scrambling through another predawn bear crawl, Zach screamed out, "You're not going to break us." I didn't know whether he was challenging me or begging for more, but I was going to find out.

Changing the culture of a team is not easy. There will always be resistance when you're demanding change. We played terribly in our first game of the 2012 season despite winning in our home stadium. A day or two later I was working at my desk when Zach and linebacker Etienne Sabino, both of whom had been elected team captains, appeared in my doorway.

"You got a minute, Coach?" Zach asked.

"Sure, what's up?"

"Well, we've been thinking and a lot of the guys feel this way, but we're practicing longer and harder than we ever have," he said. "We're lifting a lot more weights and having more physical practices than before, and we think it's why we're not playing well. During the course of the game our legs are getting tired and our shoulders are sore. By the time we get to the end of the game, we're fatigued and I think we're not playing well because we're working too hard."

I put my pencil down. I was quiet for a minute. I wanted to clarify my thoughts and evaluate the situation before I responded. I looked hard at both of them.

"No, I will tell you why you're not playing well," I said. "It's because we have a selfish, lazy team that complains all the time. We lack leadership. I told you to trust the plan and you need to do it now." I didn't hear another complaint from Zach or Etienne or anybody else. In fact, both of those guys emerged as tremendous leaders for our team.

Zach, in particular, impressed me as a guy who would do anything for his teammates. I found this out for certain in a game against Indiana at their stadium six weeks after our difficult conversation. Zach had been our starting fullback for thirty games. We had three linebackers out with injuries, and at the Tuesday practice before we had to travel to Bloomington, Indiana, I asked him how he felt about helping us by moving to the other side of the ball and playing linebacker.

"Whatever you need, Coach," he said. "I love this team, and I'll do anything to help us win."

Four days later, he had eight solo tackles and enabled us to hold off Indiana. He then stayed at linebacker for the remaining games of his career. The guy would give a limb to help the team. He was a galvanizing force who wasn't going to quit and he wasn't going to let you quit either. And every remaining day that season I watched Zach Boren bring everything he had, and bring his teammates along with him. We started out that season playing terribly, but somehow we kept finding ways to win. If the guys on that 2012 team hadn't played their hearts out, if they'd decided to give up because of what happened with the previous staff and the bowl ban and the injuries, we easily could have lost five or six games.

Never did I imagine that a group of players who started the season doing bear crawls in the ice at 5 A.M. would finish the season 12–0. Never did I imagine that this would be the group that would completely change the narrative surrounding Ohio State football and complete only the sixth undefeated season in the program's 125-year history. Never did I imagine that a group of players could change and give that kind of effort, compete with that kind of spirit, and grow closer together as brothers.

I owe them so much, and I've never forgotten that.

We take accountability seriously. We grade our players on every measure of performance possible at Ohio State. We grade their performances in games, practices, weight room, conditioning, nutrition, rehab, and, especially, in the classroom and tutor sessions. Each Thursday, every player gets a score on a scale of 1 to 10 to determine his accountability in each area. If you are in the 8 to 10 range, you've got nothing to worry about. Anything below that and you are deemed not accountable. We impose a variety of consequences, ranging from no bowl gifts or rings and loss of weight-room privileges to no letters of recommendation, and, of course, suspensions. Suffice it to say that if we aim to be Nine Units Strong and you are not contributing, there will be repercussions.

You must guard against focusing so much on wins and losses that you don't pour all the energy and clarity required to build a healthy culture. Yes, results are important. We're all in this to produce results. But again, culture is what sustains the behavior that gets you those results. Build the culture. The results will come.

||||||||||||||||||

Chapter Three: Creating a Culture Playbook

- Leaders create culture. Culture drives behavior. Behavior produces results.

- The power of culture lies in its ability to engage hearts and minds, align effort, and energize the behavior called for by your strategy.

- Nothing affects daily execution more powerfully than culture.

- The behavior of your people is a reflection of the culture you create.

- Every organization has a culture either by design or by default.

- Winning behavior will not thrive in a culture that does not support it.

||||||||||||||||||

||||||||||||||||||||||||||||||||||

FOUR

Relentless Effort

EMBRACE THE GRIND

It was 5:55 A.M. on a cold Wednesday in February 2014. We were in the team room preparing to go to mat drills. The lights had just come on after we had watched the gut-wrenching "lowlights" video of our losses to Michigan State and Clemson. I reminded our players that our culture of relentless effort is the only acceptable standard of behavior and performance.

This is what I said:

We will practice and play with relentless effort. We will go four to six seconds, point A to point B, as hard as we can. This is the culture of Ohio State football. It is what we believe and how we behave. It is who we are. It is our standard. It is how we practice and how we play. Accept nothing less from yourself. Accept nothing less from your teammates. Put your foot in the ground and go four to six, A to B, as hard as you can.

You will be graded on effort. Your unit will be graded on effort. We can teach and correct technique and execution, but the heart of our team is relentless effort. This kind of relentless effort is intentional and Above the Line. We are going to train mentally and physically so that no matter what the event is, you respond with relentless effort. In strength and conditioning. In practice. In games. Four to six. A to B. As hard as you can.

In our world, at the end of the day it is pretty simple: either you worked harder than your opponents or you got outworked. The challenge is to build a culture—a competitive environment—where everyone gives relentless effort every day. A culture everyone wants but few get.

At Ohio State, we have made relentless effort part of our DNA, and here is why: great effort can overcome poor execution, but great execution cannot overcome poor effort. Toughness and effort are the foundation of our success. I place a premium on relentless effort because in all my years of coaching, I've never been in a football game where the team that played the hardest didn't win.

One of the ways we accomplish this is by embracing what we call the grind.

Workouts at Ohio State are brutal. Coach Mick designs them that way. Our guys fully accept the challenge of effort and toughness in our workouts and practice. They understand that the ability to compete and win is forged in the crucible of training. It is forged in the grind.

We believe that being elite is not about how talented you are. It is about how tough you are. To achieve anything great in life, you have to fight for it. Every day. The grind is mental and physical. In fact, it is more mental than physical. Physical ability is important, but it will only take you so far. You won't achieve excellence until you train your mind to take you there. We demand effort, and there are consequences if you don't give it.

So we use the grind to train the mind. First you win the battle in your mind. Next you win the battle in practice. Then (and only then) you win the battle in the game.

"My job is to maximize our players' genetic potential," says Coach Mick. "We do that by increasing their work capacity beyond their physical limits. Too often the mind turns the body off. We push you to stay engaged and train your mind to work harder and longer."

An important component of his program is the mental stress he puts on players when training. He does this by adding sets and reps just when the players thought they were done, not telling them until right before the workout what the training regimen is for that day, and mixing up their training partners, among many other tactics. It's all part of the mental stress that he induces to create the chaos for players to work through and overcome. He says, "Chaos, confusion, and conflict. Our players are going to experience it on the field. It's our responsibility to train them to learn how to deal with it and rise above it."

Not all of our players come to Ohio State knowing how to

go four to six, A to B, on every play. It's something they have to learn, and every player has different trigger points. Beyond being a master at training elite athletes, Coach Mick is an expert at finding each player's motivating factor that drives him from just putting out to giving relentless effort. "It takes creating a little fear, creating a little conflict to find out what he's made of," Coach Mick says.

I want to find out in February during mat drills how tough a player is, not in November on fourth and five against Michigan State. A crucial part of winter conditioning is the mat drills Coach Mick, his assistants, and our staff put our players through in the early-morning hours throughout February. They set up stations on six large wrestling mats on our indoor field and turn the heaters up to increase the temperature. Three of the stations are one-on-one competitions with ropes, tires, and bone dummies. The other three are group agility drills involving seat rolls, bear crawls, and short sprints. Every player goes through each station at least twice in a circuit with very little rest. Every station is a mental and physical battle that induces fatigue quickly. They are designed to strip away football talent and get to the core of how tough our players are. We discover who is willing to push himself when conflict arises, who can handle chaotic situations, who backs down from confrontation, and who taps out when pressure and discomfort are applied. We find who will respond Above the Line.

The impact that Coach Mick's strength and conditioning program has had on our team is immeasurable. The key is that his training strategy must be applied consistently and with conviction. Conviction is depth of belief; consistency is the duration of it. "We absolutely believe that how we train our guys will help them reach their maximum genetic potential and we apply that belief, not just a few hard workouts a month, but every day we train. Everything we do has a purpose to benefit our players. From training to nutrition to recovery, nothing is passive. We leave nothing to chance."

The principle of relentless effort applies to everyone, not just college football players. Here's the not-so-hidden secret for achieving extraordinary success: clarify what you really want, then work as hard as you can for as long as it takes. Toughness can achieve things that talent by itself can never accomplish.

Success is cumulative and progressive. It is the result of what you do every day. Both successful and unsuccessful people take daily action. The difference is that successful people take action Above the Line. They step up and act with intention, purpose, and skill.

For every goal you are pursuing a process is involved. There is a pathway you must follow. To achieve your goals you must commit to the process with daily Above the Line behavior. Not just once or twice, but repeatedly over time. Success is not achieved by an occasional heroic response. Success is achieved by focused and sustained action. All achievement is a series of choices. The bigger the achievement, the longer the series and more challenging the choices.

Goal clarity is essential, but so is process clarity. For every goal you have set, be exceptionally clear about the process necessary to achieve the desired outcome. By acting Above the Line consistently over time you can accomplish almost anything.

Sometimes it's a grind. Sometimes tedious and uncomfortable things are required for success. And that means doing what needs to be done even though you don't feel like it. It will be uncomfortable, maybe even for long stretches, and it will be tempting to settle for an easier way that is more convenient and less difficult. But don't compromise. Don't give in. Step up and embrace the grind.

Relentless effort (not talent or intelligence) is the key to achieving great things in your life. Struggle is part of the process. It is hard and often painful. But it's also necessary, because it's in the struggle that great things are achieved.

Do you decide what to do based on what is comfortable and convenient, or based on what is productive and necessary? Following your passion isn't always 100 percent pleasurable. Sometimes it means doing things you don't want to do for the sake of achieving your goals.

If you want to win in the future, you must win the grind today. And then tomorrow and the next day and the next. Many people give up—they compromise—much too easily when life gets difficult. Be the exception and step up to the challenges you face. The grind is when it gets tedious, tiring, and difficult. But that's what separates the elite from the average. If you want to achieve any goal in your life, go four to six seconds, point A to point B, as hard as you can.

||||||||||||||||||

Michigan State was a formidable and respected opponent, and playing at their home stadium in East Lansing made the challenge of winning even tougher. There was no doubt this would be our most critical game to date, on the road against the first top ten team we'd played all season on a prime-time stage with the ESPN *GameDay* crew on hand. The Spartans had only one loss on the season—a hard-fought road game against Oregon. This Michigan State team was just as good as the team that had beaten us in the Big Ten championship the previous season, and here we were, still a young team about to face our most daunting game of the season thus far. We didn't have to state the obvious: a loss would certainly end any chance of making it into the final four for the first College Football Playoff. This was a great team we were about to play. This game would be a defining moment for our season.

I had confidence that if we executed the way we had trained, we would have a legitimate shot at winning. In the six games since the Virginia Tech defeat, we had averaged 52 points per game, and had an average margin of victory of nearly five touchdowns. But in an environment as hostile as Spartan Stadium, execution can easily give way to distraction and confusion.

To beat Michigan State, we would have to play championship-level football. Would our players rise to the occasion? Could they handle the intimidating atmosphere? Had we moved past and gotten better since last season's defeat?

What was going to get us through this game? Would we be Nine Units Strong?

Years ago, I was speaking with a friend of mine, Colonel Don Wolfe, now retired from the Army Special Forces. As we talked he told me about a quote that he and his teammates used in training and on missions. "Hold your point," he said. "What separates us from the conventional army is our mastery of the fundamentals. Because we master the basics, you don't have to worry about your teammates when things fall apart around you. We never move backward—always forward. Never give up ground and always hold your point." On missions, every special operator has an assignment and his team has strategic points that must be reached and held for the mission's success. If he holds his point, the guy to his left holds his point, the guy to his right holds his point, and every operator in the unit holds their point, they can accomplish their mission.

For us to be successful against Michigan State, we needed every player to hold his point during practice and on game day. If every player held his point, did his job with relentless effort, we had a shot at winning. Anything less against a quality opponent would result in a loss. As the days leading up to the game grew fewer, our team's level of preparation and professionalism elevated. After a close call against Penn State, our players' resilience grew stronger than even I anticipated. They had been trained well.

It was a damp and cloudy day in East Lansing, but there was a crisp chill in the air that made it just right for a prime-time football game. The day had just fully turned to night when we arrived at Spartan Stadium. During warm-ups, our guys had a nervous energy about them. They wanted to get this game started. They wanted to prove themselves.

In the locker room, our unit leaders pulled their guys in close with last-minute notes about what to expect and words of encouragement. Tom Herman gathered the offense and said, "Everybody plays hard for the men in their unit and for this offense. Opportunities multiply as they are seized. Go grab this one—they're not going to give it to you. This is going to be a four-quarter battle. Come out swinging!" Luke Fickell had the defense gathered in tight around him. "All I ask is that you play with no fear. No fear!" he said. "You play to win! Give relentless effort till the whistle blows, then get ready for the next play. No matter what comes out that gate, you stay together." Curtis Grant's speech to the defense was particularly moving. "We need every single one of y'all bringing everything y'all got, 'cause I'm gonna put it out there tonight, bro." He continued, his passion increasing with every word, "We going a hundred miles an hour tonight! We gotta win something, man, do or die tonight—do or die! This game determines the rest of our season. It's another big stage in our life we gotta tackle! I love y'all, men. Let's go!" The strain in his voice left no doubt how these players felt about each other, and if we didn't come out of this game with a win, it wouldn't be because they held back.

Michigan State took an early one-touchdown lead, and for the rest of the half it was a back-and-forth slugfest. Our issue wasn't that we weren't playing hard. I was impressed by how hard our guys were going. We just had a couple of turnovers that resulted in advantageous field position for the Spartans. On the defensive side we had done a good job of controlling the line of scrimmage, especially given the field position resulting from the fumbles, and had only given up a couple of big plays. Our passing game was working as well as it had all season. J.T. was connecting with multiple receivers with great efficiency. Devin Smith caught a 44-yard touchdown, and Michael Thomas turned a short slant route into a 79-yard touchdown after breaking a couple of tackles. J.T. and Zeke were gaining good yardage on the ground thanks to our offensive line.

Now ahead by a touchdown going into halftime, the momentum was in our favor. Our players knew the key was to keep playing with relentless effort. We made mistakes, huge mistakes, yet we were still ahead of a great team on their home ground. My message was clear and simple at halftime. "For thirty minutes you had a directive, a mission, and an assignment. You did that. Now you're getting another one, let's finish the second half. Hold your point! You keep putting your foot in the ground going four to six, A to B, as hard as you can go. You've got another directive, mission, and assignment. Get it done."

And they did. Michigan State's offense opened the second half and we held them to a field goal. Our ensuing offensive drive marched 77 yards and ended with Zeke pounding in another touchdown. After a rough first half, Eli Apple came up with one of the biggest defensive plays of the night. On the last play of the third quarter, the Spartans had fourth and five on our 35-yard line. They ran a reverse to their running back but Eli didn't take the bait and made a huge tackle for a loss. The momentum remained on our side for the duration of the game.

Our defense made great plays when it mattered most. Michael Bennett finished the night with an outstanding performance with two tackles, two tackles for loss, two pass break-ups, and a sack. Offensively, we finished with 300 yards in the air and 268 on the ground. We had a 300-yard passer (J.T.), a 100-yard rusher (Zeke), and a 100-yard receiver (Devin). You dream about offensive days like this, with every part of the offense working at near-peak efficiency.

But from a competitive standpoint, our Above the Line response to adversity and an intensity that never wavered might've been even more impressive. We made mistakes, but we never let up. Afterward, when a reporter asked me about our team, I said, "This is a different Buckeye team than it was early in the season. This team right now is playing on a very, very high level."

Our challenge was to take it even higher. It bears repeating: I've never been in a football game where the team that played the hardest didn't win.

||||||||||||||||||

Chapter Four: Relentless Effort Playbook

- The foundation of our success is relentless effort. We go four to six seconds, point A to point B, as hard as we can.

- Elite is not about how talented you are. It is about how tough you are.

- Success is cumulative and progressive. So is failure. It is the result of what you do every day.

- Relentless effort (not talent or intelligence) is the key to achieving great things in your life.

- If you want to win in the future, you must win the grind today.

||||||||||||||||||

FIVE

Competitive Excellence

THE BEST "GAMERS"

ARE THE BEST "PRACTICERS"

Elite performance requires elite preparation. It requires mental and physical reps, and we place a premium on both. Competitors have a fierce desire to win. They desire to excel and they hate to lose. They have a powerful combination of drive and discipline: the drive to do the work necessary to prepare, and the discipline to do the work right. This spirit, the spirit of a competitor, is what separates the elite from the average. We call it competitive excellence. It's about preparing mentally and physically to compete on game day so that when your number is called you're ready to make the play.

Elite competitors don't just flip the switch on game day. They understand the importance of training and practice. The mindset and attitude they bring to preparation is different from the average player. That's why I turn guys around at that red line before practice if I don't think they are ready to go.

Every day we challenge our guys: "Are you just going through the motions, or are you training to get better?" When you come to practice, you're coming to compete. This is where and when you build your competitive edge. You can't practice on autopilot and play with purpose. Autopilot is the enemy of greatness. In order to perform at the highest level on game day, you have to prepare that way throughout the week. Every player is required to be engaged in the drill. If you're not taking the physical rep, you're taking the mental rep. There are no wasted reps.

Every. Rep. Matters.

Football is a game of matchups. If you want to win the matchup—that personal battle—you have to prepare for it. It's *mano a mano*. You versus him. It's your training versus his training.

You're either a competitor with a fierce desire to be the best, or you're not.

I truly believe that the way we do things gives us a competitive advantage. Because when game day comes, when championships come, our team's level of preparation will be tested. Our players are not perfect. They fail often, but they fail forward. They make mistakes during training and fix them before it matters on the field of play. On game day, when our players are prepared, and they know they are ready, they play with great confidence and speed. Preparation stops when the foot hits the ball. Then it's about making adjustments.

Will you be ready when your number is called?

Those who watched Ohio State play in 2012 and 2013 saw it on display with Kenny Guiton. Several times in both of those seasons, Braxton Miller went down, and Kenny's number was called. It happened in the Purdue game in 2012. And again it happened in 2013, for three consecutive games. Kenny was magnificent, accounting for almost 1,000 yards of offense and throwing for twelve touchdowns.

More recently, it is what J. T. Barrett did when Braxton went down, and what Cardale Jones did when J.T. went down. People see the remarkable performances of these players on Saturday, but they do *not* see the tireless work that those players and their unit leaders put into training and preparing to compete. And they did the work not knowing when, or even if, their number would be called.

I was reminded of the value of competitive excellence while I was on the treadmill one day. I was watching an ESPN report about one of my favorite sports moments: Kirk Gibson and the famous walk-off home run he hit in the 1988 World Series off future Hall of Famer Dennis Eckersley.

The Dodgers were down a run with two outs in the ninth. With one man on base, Gibson stepped up to bat. In preparation for the game, all of the Dodger hitters were provided a detailed scouting report about the A's pitchers—what they throw, when they tend to throw it, and the tendencies they have against right- or left-handed hitters. Gibson's report said that when Eckersley gets to a 3–2 count, he always throws a backdoor slider—a pitch that breaks hard into the strike zone at the last moment.

After two consecutive strikes and three consecutive balls, the count was full. Gibson stepped up to the plate, then quickly backed out of the box for a moment. The scout's note about the backdoor slider ran through his mind.

Gibson took a moment, regripped his bat, then got back in the box and settled into his stance. Eckersley came set, then fired his sidearm offering.

It was a backdoor slider.

Kirk Gibson uncoiled, connected, and launched the ball over the right field fence. Dodgers poured out of the dugout to celebrate the franchise's first walk-off home run in World Series history. Gibson's mindful preparation, thanks to a well-prepared scouting report, won the game and helped win the Series for the Los Angeles Dodgers.

Kenny Guiton and Kirk Gibson are two of the best examples of competitive excellence I can think of. I tell these stories and show the video clips to my players every year. If you passed Taylor Decker or any other Buckeye on the street and said, "Backdoor slider," he'd smile and know exactly what you were talking about. Elite performers don't get to that level by accident, but through great coaching and careful attention to preparation.

In the hours and days following Super Bowl XLIX, there were numerous interviews with Malcolm Butler, the New England Patriots' cornerback, who had produced what instantly became one of the most heroic plays in Super Bowl history. His story was such a clear example of competitive excellence that we use it as another one of our primary reference points when teaching our players. We streamed Butler's commentary throughout the facility for all the players to see and learn from.

In the final seconds of the game, New England is leading Seattle, 28–24, but the Seahawks are on the 1-yard line, second and goal. Butler, a free agent out of the University of West Alabama, is in the defensive backfield for the Patriots. When the Seahawks break the huddle, they stack two receivers to the right. Butler has instant recognition of what the Seahawks are planning.

"I remembered the formation they were in, two receivers stacked, I just knew they were going to [run a] pick route," Butler said.

In the days leading up to the big game, Butler had studied numerous hours of Seahawks' film. The Patriots scout team had run the play in practice multiple times. And now, his number had been called.

The Seahawks' quarterback takes the snap, makes a quick

drop, looks and passes right. Butler explodes forward. He beats the receiver to the ball, making the interception and clinching the Super Bowl victory.

It was an outstanding play, and you know what made it even more brilliant? Two plays earlier, on a long pass play down the right sideline, Butler's man made a crazy, flat-on-his-back catch, even though Butler had deflected the ball and had apparently broken up the play. Butler later used the word "devastated" to describe his emotional state in that moment. He thought he had lost the Super Bowl for his team. And then look at what Malcolm Butler did. He managed that horrific event as well as you can manage it. He turned his focus to making his response the best it could be. Like Kirk Gibson, he pressed pause and got his mind right. He changed the only thing he could change—how he performed on the very next play.

He did his job brilliantly. It was the definition of competitive excellence.

The most anticipated game of every season at Ohio State is the one against That Team Up North. It is, after all, not *a* game. It is *the* game. It is why we played LL Cool J's "It's Time for War" on an endless loop in the Woody Hayes Athletic Center the entire week beforehand. Every year this game is a battle. It is the greatest rivalry in sports.

"The great thing about this game is one team could not have won a game all year and the other one can be undefeated," Joshua Perry said, "but you never know what's going to come out the gate. That's why you play it, that's why you enjoy it and why you prepare."

There was no preparing for the first play of the fourth quarter, however. We were leading by a touchdown, 28–21. Ezekiel Elliott had just run for 9 yards to give us a second-and-one on our own 33-yard line. J. T. Barrett took the ball and started right, faking a handoff to Zeke, then cutting back to get the first down himself. He got stopped cold by three defenders for no gain. As the players untangled from the pile, J.T. remained on the ground. Our trainers ran out to attend to him. J.T. still was not up. Now I was getting worried. When you see medical staff huddling around a player, it is never good news. His ankle was broken. His remarkable freshman season was done, just like that.

One teammate after another went over to J.T. as he lay on the ground at our 33-yard line. His message was the same to all of them.

"Win this game," he said. In terrible pain, all J.T. was focused on was the team. What a special leader that young man is. After a few minutes, J.T. was helped up and lifted onto a cart. Curtis Grant came over and hugged him. A few other guys did the same, offered words of encouragement. J.T. waved to the crowd as he was carted off.

The next man up was Cardale Jones, a six-foot five-inch, 250-pound sophomore from Cleveland, our third-string quarterback. He had thrown fourteen passes all season, nearly all of them in blowout victories. Now he was our starter and would be for the rest of the year. This is where all the reps in practice and all the focus on competitive excellence come into play. Would he be ready? Would the offense respond? Would we get through an unexpectedly tight game and get to next week's Big Ten championship game against Wisconsin with our undefeated conference season intact?

It was still a one-score game with just over five minutes to go when we had the ball on That Team Up North's 44. It was fourth and one. Our College Football Playoff aspirations could well be riding on this play. Failing to convert here would give our rival a short field and a good deal of momentum. I called a timeout and the offense jogged to the sideline as Tom Herman and I ran through the possibilities.

Huddled around me, I looked at the offensive linemen. All of them.

I looked Ed Warinner right in the eyes and sternly asked, "Can you get the first down?"

Without a split second of doubt or hesitation, he replied, "We can get it!"

His linemen chimed in and I heard in all of their voices the same confidence as their unit leader, "We got this! We can get it!"

We decided to go with a split-zone play, with receiver Jalin Marshall in the backfield with Zeke and Cardale, a formation that we hadn't used all season. The play calls for a blocking scheme that we typically use for short-yardage quarterback keepers, and we figured the opponent would expect us to give the ball to our 250-pound quarterback to pound away for the yard. Just before the snap, tight end Nick Vannett went in motion behind the line. When Cardale took the snap, the offensive line zone blocked to the right as Cardale handed the ball off to Zeke, who pressed into the line of scrimmage and cut back to his left. Taylor Decker forced the left defensive end away from the gap and Vannett took care of the unblocked right defensive end who had stayed home to guard against a Cardale run, just as we'd hoped. Everyone was doing his job. Zeke broke a tackle at the line of scrimmage and was gone, untouched, into the end zone. We were up by two scores, and soon it was three when Darron Lee recovered a fumble caused by Joey Bosa and ran it in for a touchdown.

We were heading back to Indianapolis for another Big Ten championship game, this time against Wisconsin, a powerful team with one of the best running backs in the country: Melvin Gordon. J.T.'s injury confronted us with a very difficult event, and we responded. It was what our players had been trained to do. It was what they'd been prepared to do. Our winning streak stood at ten games. We started preparing for Wisconsin the next day. However, there are some things in life you can simply never prepare for. The day after we beat That Team Up North, Sunday of Thanksgiving weekend, was one of them.

I was on the practice field when I got the news.

Kosta Karageorge, one of our walk-on players, had taken his own life.

A big, strong young man who had been a very good heavyweight wrestler for Ohio State and had just joined the team in August, Kosta had not shown up for practice the previous Wednesday. It was not like him at all, but I had no reason initially to think anything terrible had happened. I can't say that I knew him well, but he always seemed upbeat. I used to call him "The Mad Greek." I'd ask him how he was doing and he'd answer the same way every time:

"I'm doing great, Coach."

Kosta enjoyed being part of the team. The guys really took to him. He was a hard worker and brought an energetic presence on the defensive line unit. When he didn't show up on Thursday or Friday, I became much more alarmed. We had no clue what was going on. We just hoped we'd see him back in his No. 53 jersey soon. When we took the field at Ohio Stadium, on Senior Day, twenty-three players were saluted on the occasion of their last home game. Kosta Karageorge's photo appeared on the video screen along with a plea for help finding him.

Columbus police were investigating but hadn't turned up any leads except for some text messages he had sent to his mother. I didn't know what was going on. I just knew this wasn't good. The police kept looking. On Sunday, a 9-1-1 call came in. Police responded and raced over to check out a Dumpster in a Columbus neighborhood about a tenth of a mile from Kosta's apartment.

It was where they found Kosta's body.

When I called the team together and told them the tragic news after practice, nobody wanted to believe it. We had a moment of silence on the field for Kosta and his family. Soon the tributes poured in.

"He was a fun guy," offensive tackle Taylor Decker said. "Easy to be around. A blue-collar American guy. It's just sad. A huge team guy. I have a lot of respect for him as a person."

Joshua Perry said: "He was one of the hardest-working guys I ever knew. He was lighthearted and always had a smile on his face. We are praying for his family."

Michael Bennett, a defensive lineman and captain, said he was going to wear Kosta's No. 53 for the rest of the season. The next day there was a press conference in advance of the Big Ten title game, and it was impossible to think about football. I kept thinking about Kosta's parents and what they must be going through. A reporter asked me about how I was dealing with Kosta's passing.

"It's difficult. You can look in a coaching manual, I'm not sure you'll find anything. . . . We'll never get over it," I said.

I prayed for the young man and prayed for his family. I knew Larry Johnson, our defensive line coach and a deeply spiritual man, would be looking out for his guys, urging them to share their feelings and deal with their loss. You try to make sense of it and, as a person of faith, try to understand how God would have it end this way for this young man. It was what I kept thinking about when we attended his funeral, a week after he had disappeared. More than anything, my heart broke for him and his family.

I keep asking why, and I get nowhere. I just pray that the family can find the strength to cope with their loss, and that Kosta Karageorge is at peace.

||||||||||||||||||

As difficult as it was in the wake of this tragedy, we had a Big Ten championship game to prepare for. Like us, Wisconsin had an early nonconference loss but had won seven straight games and was a formidable opponent, particularly with the emergence of Melvin Gordon as one of the best running backs in the country. My primary focus going in was to get Cardale comfortable and to put him in a position to succeed. He is a young man with all the talent in the world, but he was about to start his first college football game with a championship at stake—a much bigger stage than Cleveland's Glenville High School, where he played for the legendary Ted Ginn, Sr.

Our mindset going into the game was to minimize risk and make sure Cardale understood that just because he was taking over for J.T. didn't mean he had to be a one-man show for us. One of the biggest dangers in such a situation is for a player to try to do too much. When a kid puts that kind of pressure on himself, he usually winds up being tight and underperforming. You don't have to be Braxton Miller or J. T. Barrett—just be the best Cardale Jones you can be. That was the essence of Tom Herman's message to him all week.

"The quarterback doesn't have to win games for us, the quarterback has to manage games and distribute the football and lead," Tom said. "We've seen that throughout this season. As long as Cardale's mentally prepared and he's got a ton of physical tools . . . I have nothing but the utmost confidence in him because of what we've got around him."

As the game approached, my biggest question about Cardale was from a leadership perspective. I've seen him throw a ball 75 yards flat-footed. After practice one day, he told one of our guys, "Watch this," and then popped a guy on the helmet from 50 yards away. I've seen him run over guys and then run away from them, all on the same play. The guy has it all, but it was maturity and his mental approach I was less sure about. This was his third year in the program, and I still had doubts because of the way he handled himself at times. One day he didn't tape his ankles before practice. You have to tape your ankles; everybody does. And the time that he didn't, he rolled his ankle two days before a game. I was so angry with him. Everybody was. It was just how Cardale was at times. He was fundamentally a good guy but just wasn't serious-minded about his work, a player who would often goof around in practice and the weight room. If something went wrong—if he showed up late for a meeting or messed up a read in practice—he always had a ready excuse. Excuses don't get you anyplace around here. If you screw up, I don't want your explanation, and I don't want drama. I want your ownership. So for all he had going for him, I needed to see him emerge as a leader.

It's one thing to take snaps from center. It's another thing to be a quarterback.

Our offensive game plan was to play outside the hashes in our passing game. We did not want to take the chances of tipped balls or high throws, which are not uncommon with young quarterbacks who might be fighting some nerves. Wisconsin had the No. 2-ranked pass defense in the country. Starting this way, we thought we could move the ball and build some confidence in Cardale, and then take some downfield shots on their corners—just not over the middle. They were a man coverage team, and with the weapons we had on the outside, especially Devin Smith and Michael Thomas, we liked our chances with those matchups. We'd averaged 44 points over the previous five games and had no doubt we could move the ball, no matter who we were playing, and it sure didn't hurt that Cardale had the best tutor he could've had: J. T. Barrett.

Not even four months earlier, it was J.T. who was the untested kid, taking over after Braxton Miller went down with his shoulder injury. J.T. could not have been a better teammate or leader. He helped Cardale with his film study, with his reads, with his mental reps. He boosted him at every turn. We had committed so much time and focus to building the brotherhood of trust, and here it was in action. Here was J. T. Barrett investing in his brother and putting his unit and his team before himself.

"I feel like his world is probably like mine was at the beginning of the year. If anybody knows what that feels like, I definitely do," J.T. said. "But Cardale's a great player. I honestly feel like if I wasn't starting this year, Cardale would've done the same things that I did because Cardale's that talented.

"My main thing was to make sure his nerves were calm. I learned that myself—you've got to get the jitters out. I knew he'd be great. I told him I'd be there. I wanted to be the one he could talk to."

|||||||||||||||||||

On the first play from scrimmage, Cardale rolled right and hit Michael Thomas for an 8-yard pickup. A couple of plays later he fired to Corey Smith on a quick-hitting slant for nine more. After a couple of runs by Zeke, Cardale stayed calmly in the pocket and threw a 39-yard touchdown pass to Devin Smith in the end zone. He was three-for-three for 56 yards on the first drive of his life as an Ohio State starter. It was a pretty fair way to break in. On our next set of downs we went three-and-out, and it showed me more than the touchdown drive did.

From our own 30-yard line, we had a third-and-fourteen when Cardale dropped back and threw a deep pass over the middle for Jalin Marshall, right into double coverage. It was exactly what he was told not to do. The pass was nearly intercepted. When he came back to the sideline, I was ready to jump him and demand an explanation. Before I could say a word, Cardale came straight up to me.

"My bad, Coach," he said. "I know I wasn't supposed to do that. It won't happen again."

I was stunned. Cardale had been hearing about accountability, staying Above the Line, and not falling into BCD behavior for a couple of years. Until that moment, I wasn't sure the message had ever gotten through.

"What did you say?" I asked.

"I said, 'My bad.' I shouldn't have thrown that ball."

115

I wanted to hug him.

"I want you to go over there and tell your offensive lineman just what you told me," I said.

And he did.

Cardale wasn't just taking snaps anymore. He was a quarterback.

"The minute I released the ball, I knew I shouldn't have," Cardale said. "I thought, 'Why did I just do that?' It was just a brain fart. I was being greedy, I guess. When I jogged off the field, I had my head up, looking for Coach. I knew what was coming. This was the position I always wanted to be in. Now I had the role I wanted, but you have to understand what comes with it. You have to take ownership of things. You have to be there for your teammates. That's all I was trying to do."

The most rewarding moments for me as a leader come when you see somebody finally get it, when you see growth and maturity. However, in this case I don't think his transformation had much to do with my leadership. I think it had to do with the brotherhood, and Cardale wanting to be a trustworthy warrior for his team. Having Cardale own that incomplete pass was one of the most gratifying things that happened the whole season. What a difference it made in that game, in our ability to keep pushing forward.

And that is what we did, with unrelenting intensity, the entire game against Wisconsin. Melvin Gordon was carrying the ball behind a line that averaged six feet six inches and 320 pounds and came in averaging 188 yards and 8 yards per carry. Two weeks earlier, he'd run for 408 yards and four touchdowns against Nebraska. This was the epitome of a power team in the championship of a power conference. We knew the game would be won or lost at the line of scrimmage. Their whole running game was based on double-teaming our line and opening holes for Gordon to explode through. We talked all week about "gap integrity," which means fighting off the block and owning your gap. If everybody owned their gap, Gordon would get his yards but we would eliminate the big plays. We were so committed to not letting Gordon beat us that we put nine guys in the box and dared them to try to take us on in the air.

We controlled the line of scrimmage from start to finish. Everyone on the defensive side of the ball was tremendous. They were truly warriors. They'd been training for this for months, starting in the weight room back in January, embracing the grind, driving themselves through pain and fatigue, and here was the payoff. It didn't happen because they had the good fortune to play a good game. It happened because they are elite athletes who trained to do exactly this. Up front, Joey Bosa and Michael Bennett led the attack, winning their battles again and again. Bennett alone had four tackles for loss and two sacks. The dominant play of the line enabled the linebackers, led by Darron Lee and Curtis Grant, to make key stops, and on the rare occasions that Gordon had any room our defensive backs were superb in their tackling and not letting him go for a big gain. Melvin Gordon wound up with 76 yards on twenty-six carries, not even 3 yards per rush. Ten of his carries went for either losses or no gain.

For three hours that December night, I looked out on the

field and saw guys who refused to lose, and refused to make any excuses for their hardships. It was incredible to watch. From a leadership standpoint, I try to help guys understand that sometimes the problem isn't the problem. Sometimes, the bigger issue is how you respond to the problem. You build resilience by training and developing your ability to respond long before adversity ever hits.

When you win a game 59–0, it's impossible to single anybody out as the difference maker. Cardale played a phenomenal game with no turnovers and three touchdown passes. Zeke ran for 220 yards, including an 81-yard touchdown run. Devin Smith caught three touchdown passes. The lines on both sides were magnificent. But for a highlight, it was hard to beat the play right before halftime. Deep in his own territory, Gordon ran left, where Michael Bennett slammed into him, knocking the ball loose. Bosa scooped it up and dove into the end zone. It made the score 37–0, but that wasn't what made it special. Michael Bennett made the play in his new jersey, No. 53. He was wearing it in honor of the teammate he dedicated the game to: Kosta Karageorge.

||||||||||||||||

Chapter Five: Competitive Excellence Playbook

- You will play like you practice. You can't practice on autopilot and play with purpose. How you compete in practice will determine how you compete in games.

- Elite performance requires elite preparation.

- Developing skill requires lots of reps. Physical and mental reps. Every rep counts.

- You never know when your opportunity will come. The key is to be prepared.

||||||||||||||||

SIX

|||||||||||||||||||||||||||||||||||||||

Power of the Unit

THE BROTHERHOOD OF TRUST AND

COMBAT MOTIVATION

L inebacker Joshua Perry and I were talking one day when the subject turned to the issue of trust and the connection he felt to his Ohio State teammates.

"You can't play football by yourself," Joshua said. "It is the greatest team sport. You have to be able to count on each other, trust each other completely, and know that the guy next to you will have your back, no matter what. Without that trust, you're not going to be able to do much of anything. With that trust, you can accomplish more than you can even imagine."

The task of building this trust—a bond so strong that it inspires people to give everything they have for the sake of the team—is one of the most important jobs facing any leader. I call it "solving the mystery," and it is something that I constantly focus on and think about. The mystery is this:

What motivates a player to give maximum effort and play with selfless commitment to the team?

I believe the key to solving the mystery lies in something called small-unit cohesion. The military has the same challenge we do, except they call it combat motivation. What motivates soldiers to engage in combat? How do you train soldiers to fight and win? And how do you train and equip soldiers to sustain combat motivation during periods of prolonged conflict?

Research by the U.S. military on battlefield experience has revealed that even when confronted by an attacking enemy, many soldiers hesitate to fight. The stress of battle, the fear of death, and the natural hesitancy to shoot another person all combine to produce low levels of combat motivation and thus poor battlefield performance. However, a person will fight for the guys in his unit. Tenaciously. For however long it takes.

An article by U.S. Army Major Robert J. Reilly in the November–December 2000 issue of *Military Review* spells it out very clearly. Writes Reilly, "The strongest motivation for enduring combat, especially for U.S. soldiers, is the bond formed among members of a squad or platoon. This cohesion is the single most important sustaining and motivating force for combat soldiers. Simply put, soldiers fight because of the other members of their small unit."

Unit cohesion is the bond, the deep interpersonal connection, created among the members of the unit. The most effective combat units have an uncommon commitment to each other that is built through training and then through combat itself. The unit becomes a family. The guys in the unit become a band of brothers. Soldiers fight for each other. This is the heart of combat motivation. It is the "power of the unit," a term coined by my former offensive coordinator, Steve Addazio.

G. K. Chesterton said it well:

The true soldier fights not because he hates what is in front of him, but because he loves what is behind him.

It is for this reason that we emphasize and invest in the power of the unit. We work tirelessly at building this mindset in our coaches and players. Our team is organized into nine units, with each unit led by a unit leader. We require the unit leaders to equip their players with R Factor skills and trust tools in order to build and strengthen the cohesion in their unit room. With his toolbox filled, it is the unit leader's job to get his unit to perform at maximum capacity.

With more than one hundred guys on the team, I am limited as to the number of personal touch points that I can have with players on a daily basis. But the unit leader is constantly in touch with his players. Therefore, it is the responsibility of the unit leader to make the standards of our culture clear to every player in his room, and get every player to fully commit and buy in.

I lead the team through the unit leaders.

We require our unit leaders to be exceptional teachers. Not tellers. Teachers. It is the job of the unit leader to develop his players and make them better. We want our coaches to teach four to six, A to B, with intensity and teach execution with precision. It is vitally important that the unit leaders teach both. One without the other won't work.

This is what happened in 2014. We achieved small-unit cohesion. We maximized the power of the unit. Our guys were motivated to play because of their love for each other and their love for their coaches. We were Nine Units Strong.

We solved the mystery.

Trust is something that every team talks about and wants, but few truly get. Trust is belief in the reliability of a person. It is confidence that you can count on a person. But the trust we seek to build at Ohio State goes deeper than that. It is the kind of trust that the Navy SEALs have for each other, the kind that is earned over time as guys demonstrate they can be counted on in difficult—even extreme—conditions. You do not make it through SEAL training without the support and encouragement of the guys around you. It is in the crucible of training that the bond—the uncommon commitment—of the SEAL brotherhood is built.

Exceptional teams are built on a foundation of deep trust. In order to train and compete at an elite level, you must push each other hard. Very hard. But you can push only to the level of trust you have built with each other and with your coaches. Deep trust creates a very special brotherhood. It creates an unbreakable bond among players and coaches. Trust takes the team to a level of performance that cannot be achieved without it. The strength of a team is determined by the strength of the connections on the team. A great team requires great relationships.

|||||||||||||||||||

It was a cold, gray morning in February 2014. I sat in my office and thought about how the previous season had ended. I thought about the painful losses to Michigan State and Clemson. It was clear we had a problem. We weren't Nine Units Strong, and when we played teams with equal talent we lost. How did that happen? What was missing?

In order to answer those questions I had to take a hard look at myself, our staff, and our team. The typical reaction is to blame and complain, and that often results in the head coach firing somebody. But I was determined not to do that because I knew in my heart there was a better way. That kind of self-evaluation is not easy to do. It takes time, effort, and courage. I had to get beyond the symptoms, look deep, and identify root causes.

I talked to graduating senior players and those who were moving on early to the NFL. I had one-on-one conversations with our coaching staff. I talked at length with Coach Mick. I had a deep conversation with Tim Kight. As a result of those conversations, it became evident that the root of our problem was low trust and lack of connection in some of our units.

We identified the problem, and now we needed the solution—a systematic method to teach and build trust within our units. Working with Tim, we designed a six-week series of workshops for our coaches with a specific focus on how to build trust. The core message was very straightforward: trust is earned through your behavior, not granted by your position.

And it is earned through repeated behavior over time. Every day, through your actions, you make deposits into or withdrawals from your "trust account" with the players you are seeking to lead and coach.

The framework we used is illustrated below. Trust is earned through how you behave in three areas: character, competence, and connection. All three are essential. It's the combination of the three that makes trust happen. Strength in one dimension will not compensate for weakness in another. You build credibility and earn trust with players by giving them repeated experience over time in all three dimensions.

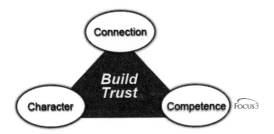

- Character is ethical trust. It is built through repeated experience of you doing what you say you will do.

- Competence is technical trust. It is built through repeated experience of you doing your job and making the team better.

- Connection is personal trust. It is built through repeated experience of you caring, listening, and fully engaging with the people on the team.

It is important to remember that players do not experience your intentions; they experience your behavior. If players are going to trust you, they must experience your character and competence, and they must experience a personal connection with you. Repeatedly. Over time. Especially in difficult conditions.

In June and July of 2014, we taught the same trust principles to our players. Every week for six weeks we met as a team, heard briefly from Tim Kight about one of the elements of trust, and watched a video that illustrated the principle. The team meetings were helpful, but the high-impact lessons on how to build trust took place following the team meeting when the players went back to their respective unit rooms. Each unit leader led his guys through an in-depth discussion of the trust principle for that particular week. What does it really mean? Why does it matter? How are you going to apply it to earn the trust of your teammates and coaches?

We kept going. That summer, in addition to the teaching on trust, each unit leader connected with his guys by having them over to his home for dinner, doing a community service project together, and taking a day for a fun outing like paintball, ziplining, or boating and tubing on the lake.

And during all of that time, our guys were training under the supervision of Coach Mick and our strength staff. The players trained in their units. They hit the grind area with their units. They encouraged each other as they suffered through ridiculously hard workouts. They pushed each other. They coached each other. They made each other better.

During our preseason camp in August of 2014, we invited Lieutenant Colonel Daniel Harris of the Army National Guard to address our team. Harris had recently returned from deployment in Kuwait, and he spoke to our players about how the Army trains and prepares soldiers for combat. It was firsthand testimony from an Army officer that confirmed our commitment to the power of the unit was right on target.

> *When our soldiers engage the enemy, when contact is made and the bullets start flying, it all comes down to training and how much our guys trust each other. We train relentlessly to fight and win. And we train in squads, which are small units. In addition to our training, what is critical to our success in combat is how much the guys in a squad trust each other and their sergeant. They build that trust in training, and they build it by spending personal time together and getting to know each other.*

At the end of his presentation, Lieutenant Colonel Harris challenged our players by reemphasizing the heart of his message: "Remember, guys, when contact is made and the bullets start flying, it all comes down to training and how much you trust each other."

The cumulative impact of all these efforts was an unbreakable bond, a true brotherhood of trust. And as the season progressed, we solved the mystery. Our guys gave maximum effort and played with selfless commitment to each other. And every unit operated at maximum capacity. We became Nine Strong.

As our team experienced adversity throughout the season,

the brotherhood of trust got deeper, growing stronger week by week. By the time we reached the postseason, the 2014 Buckeyes became one of the most closely knit teams I have ever been around. I am convinced that this unique bond was the fuel that energized our championship run. It would not have happened without the enormous investment we made in teaching and building trust among our coaches and players.

The power of the unit is no different from one of the most powerful human instincts on earth: love of family. Most of us will do anything for our families. If you come after my family, you are going to have to go through me. And there is no chance you can do that. If it comes down to it, you are going to have to kill me because I will lay down my life for them without hesitation. You do anything—and you stop at nothing—to protect your family. That is as deep a core belief as I have, and it was the same way back in the old country for my grandmother.

My mother used to tell me stories about her family and growing up in what became East Germany after World War II. She told us that when the Soviets came in they seized everything they could get their grubby Communist fingers on, whether it was a business, a bank, or a prominent person. One of the prominent people they grabbed was my grandfather, Horst Gumpert. He was the mayor of the town and the owner of a prosperous business, and the next thing my grandmother knew, her husband was hauled off to a Soviet work camp, where he was basically starved to death. He left home weighing more than two hundred pounds. They sent him back home to East Germany when he became gravely ill, maybe a year later. He weighed less than one hundred pounds. He died not long after. My mother was about twelve years old at the time. The whole family had obviously been through a terrible trauma, but my grandmother was going to do whatever she had to do to protect her family. Several days after losing her husband, she grabbed my mom and her brother, stuffed a few possessions into pillowcases, and then they all waded across a small river and crawled underneath barbed wire to get into West Germany. My mother stayed in Europe for seven more years, spending time in Germany, Austria, Italy, and England. She went to hotel school and saved up enough money to emigrate to America, and eventually a new life.

My mother used to tell me that her vision of America was freedom, beaches, and palm trees. At least she was right about the freedom. When her ship—called *Bremen*—pulled into New York Harbor, my mother's heart soared at the sight of the Statue of Liberty. As she got closer to shore, her heart was still beating fast when her nose got a whiff of maybe the worst thing she had ever smelled. Turned out New York was in the middle of a garbage strike, and there were enough piles of garbage at the edge of New York Harbor to fill the Black Forest.

"There were rats as big as Volkswagens," my mother told me. And there wasn't a palm tree in sight.

So much of the brotherhood of trust is developed based on the amount of time invested with those you care about. There is no substitute for it. I was at a Mass one time at Queen of Peace Church in Gainesville, Florida. Maddie Marotti, the daughter of Coach Mick and his wife, Susie, was getting confirmed. The bishop presiding over the service got up in the pulpit and said, "Do you know how to spell love?" People started spelling it, and the bishop stopped them. "You spell love T-I-M-E," he said.

The bishop's message resonated with me immediately, and it was conveyed to our unit leaders. For there to be a deep connection, you have to spend time with your players. They have to feel your commitment to them, experience your concern on a daily basis. That's when we initiated the social outings and barbeques. We instructed our unit coaches to start every meeting by talking for five or ten minutes about things other than football. We encouraged them to ask their players about their lives away from football, and learn about their families and girlfriends and schoolwork. We wanted the players to get to know the coaches' wives and kids, and vice versa. Beyond this intentional effort, we also wanted our unit leaders to accentuate positives. Don't just point out all the things guys do wrong. Praise them for the things they do right. Luke Fickell made it a point to finish up every meeting on a positive note to make sure his players departed in a good frame of mind.

"We all want perfection," Luke said. "That's the ultimate goal for all of us. Sometimes, though, in pursuit of that, there's too much focus on the negatives. It's not about relaxing things or lowering our standards. It's just recognizing that if we're going to put these guys under such pressure and in such hard situations, let's not forget to be positive, too. We are all seeking positives. So at the end of meeting, when they are about to leave, put something good in their head, building on what we're asking them to do. It doesn't just help guys feel good about themselves. In the long run, it allows us to push them even harder."

Joe Burger, one of our linebackers, noticed a big shift in how unit leaders interacted with their players in 2014.

"Coach Fickell talked to us so much more about the process than the final destination," Burger said. "He became more positive about everything we did, and that spilled over onto the practice field every day. It wasn't just getting through the week anymore. It was enjoying the week. Sure we had a winning streak going and we were going for a title, but the focus every day was on working as hard as we could and getting better tomorrow than we were today."

I can't think of a player who has been more transformed by the brotherhood of trust than Curtis Grant. Four years ago, Curtis was a five-star recruit from Richmond, Virginia, who was ranked as the No. 2 college prospect in the whole country, behind only Jadeveon Clowney. Everybody in the world wanted him. Jim Tressel got him, and Buckeye fans were all set to root for the latest in their team's long line of standout linebackers, from Chris Spielman to James Laurinaitis, A. J. Hawk to Pepper Johnson.

At six feet three inches and 220 pounds, Curtis could run

like a tailback and hit like a defensive end. He and Ryan Shazier, now with the Pittsburgh Steelers, were going to be as good a tandem of linebackers as there was in the country.

And then, things happened. Curtis Grant didn't produce the results we had expected from him for three years. He had various injuries. He lost his starting job three games into his sophomore year. He had an average junior season, though he dealt bravely with the tragic death of his father. He also became a father in his own right late in his career. But something was holding him back. Curtis was doing the work; he just wasn't going hard. He wasn't practicing and playing with the selflessness and strain our culture demands.

Curtis's senior year was one of the most remarkable turnarounds I have ever seen in one of my players, particularly because it happened so late in his career. Curtis wasn't merely a solid linebacker, he became the heart and soul of our defense and brought the rest of the linebackers with him. His transformation could not have happened without developing that level of trust, that small-unit cohesion, with the linebacker corps and his unit leader.

"Sometimes when people are negative, you start believing it," Curtis said. "There's a lot of nagging, and you feel like you're getting chopped down. When somebody really cares about you and they show you that they care, you're going to do whatever you can for them."

Curtis knew that he was surrounded by people who genuinely cared about him and his family. He had developed such a deep bond with his unit that his priorities shifted from worrying about his own playing time to building up the overall effectiveness of his unit. Raekwon McMillan was a highly recruited true freshman who showed early on that he could play middle linebacker his first year and compete with Curtis for playing time. Setting aside his own self-interests, Curtis began working with Raekwon during the summer, running him through drills and teaching him the nuances of our defense. The selflessness that Curtis exhibited, placing the unit and the team ahead of his chance to be a starter, is what helped build the linebackers into one of the highest performing units in our program.

He solved the mystery and so did Devin Smith, who is not just a tremendous receiver but also a superb special-teams player. His job is to evade defenders, sprint down the field, and disrupt the return. Devin does it with no fear.

A couple of years ago against Wisconsin, we had to punt at a critical time late in the game, and we needed to have great coverage on the kick. Wisconsin knew that Devin was our gunner, the guy they had to stop, so they double-teamed him. It didn't matter. He juked them and blew by them so fast they didn't even touch him. Devin defeated the blockers, raced down the field, disrupted and rerouted the returner. That gave Devin's teammates the opportunity to tackle the return man inside the 10-yard line. Devin was not credited with the tackle. His effort didn't make ESPN's highlight reel. Nevertheless, Devin Smith gave everything he had to make a critical play when it mattered most. He solved the mystery.

|||||||||||||||||||

A great example of the impact of the power of the unit is our offensive line, under the direction of coach Ed Warinner. Ed was hired in early 2012 and had a big job ahead of him. The linemen needed a lot of work in order to adjust to our new offensive system, but I knew if anyone could be a difference maker, it would be Ed. He is an exceptional coach. He connects with his players. He is disciplined and demanding and is great at earning their trust. He teaches them and he pushes them very hard. In 2014, under his leadership, the offensive line got progressively better every week. We are an offensive line–based offense. It has been a point of emphasis for me ever since I became a head coach. In order for our offense to perform well, our offensive line must perform at the highest level. There can be no weak links. There can be no weak trust among them.

Reid Fragel was a six-foot eight-inch tight end who was underachieving in the classroom and underperforming on the field. We needed a right tackle, and Ed and I agreed that if Reid could put on enough weight by the season, he might have a shot at starting. But first, we had to address the issue of whether we could trust him. We called Reid and his parents in to explain the situation and what moves we were looking to make. It was a hard, unpleasant conversation about Reid's poor academic status. The Fragels are wonderful people, but he had misled them about his grades. Tears were shed, but the truth healed those wounds quickly, and Ed went to work building a right tackle. Directed by Coach Mick, Reid gained the fifty pounds he needed while at the same time learning his new job under the tutelage of Coach Warinner.

One of the first things Coach Warinner did after his initial evaluation of his new players was assign them a position so they could own that role. For example, Corey Linsley had long been a guard until Warinner moved him to center and kept him there. "Once we decided what position they were going to play," Warinner said, "we kept them there so there would be no confusion about roles and responsibilities. Once we got them proficient enough to own their position, they could begin to master it."

Reid had never played offensive line. And with the first game of the season approaching quickly, Coach Warinner first had to understand how best to teach him. Reid, along with a few other linemen, tended to learn better with walk-throughs on the field rather than on the board in their unit room. So Ed made it a priority to be on the practice field fifteen minutes before the rest of the team so they could work on footwork and all the technical nuances that would maximize their ability to master the concepts.

But where Warinner's brilliance truly shone through was in his ability to build a sustainable brotherhood among his guys. It started with demanding discipline and respect. He holds his guys accountable for how they perform in the classroom and on the football field, and he expects them to hold each other accountable as well. But without the right support, accountability is difficult to enforce and still maintain trust. Warinner's older players help the younger ones not only with drills and techniques, but also with learning the standards and assimilating into the brotherhood.

Warinner makes sure that every Thursday night for team meal his players are eating with his wife. He frequently has them over to the house, and on game days the linemen sit together for the pregame meal.

By the end of the 2012 season, the right tackle position that had been a question mark in training camp was now one of the strengths in that unit. In fact, Reid's standout games were against two of the tougher opponents that season: Michigan State and Nebraska. In the spring of 2013, Reid Fragel was drafted by the Cleveland Browns.

Coach Warinner did it again with four more linemen—Corey Linsley, Andrew Norwell, Marcus Hall, and Jack Mewhort. They had similar story lines to Reid's—low performance on and off the field—but with Warinner's leadership and the brotherhood he built in his unit room, three of them became rookie starters in the NFL after graduating.

Every year, Warinner's line has been the anchor unit of our offense. I never had a 1,000-yard rusher in a season until 2012, when Braxton Miller rushed for over 1,200 yards. In 2013, the offense averaged more than 6 yards per carry, and Warinner's unit produced two 1,000-yard rushers with Braxton Miller and Carlos Hyde. And again in 2014, his unit enabled Ezekiel Elliott to rush for more than 1,800 yards and finish the year with a remarkable performance in the postseason. While yardage stats are great, there is an overlooked stat that is even more telling about Warinner's ability to coach sound fundamentals. In the entire 2014 season, Warinner's unit had only two holding penalties. Not per game. Only two holding penalties for the entire season. That is an amazing achievement that tells you how technically competent our guys were. Our offensive line continues to perform at a high level, and we can thank Ed Warinner for that.

There are a lot of intimidating places to play in the country. Beaver Stadium in State College, Pennsylvania, on a Saturday night prime-time game is at the top of the list, with more than 107,000 fans wearing white and making so much noise the ground shakes. It is not the type of atmosphere you'd choose for your freshman quarterback. But a few minutes after midnight in late October, J. T. Barrett showed me just how powerful the brotherhood of trust can be.

We were up 17–0 at halftime when Coach Mick and our team doctors told me that J.T. had suffered a second-degree MCL (medial collateral ligament) sprain in his knee on the last play of the half and might not be able to continue, depending on his pain threshold. Mick and I went over to talk to J.T. and tell him what the doctors said. The conversation didn't get far.

"There's no way I'm coming out of this game," he said. "I'm good, Coach. There's no way I'm letting my teammates down. I am going to go out there and win this game." The ultimate decision doesn't rest with the player. The medical staff has the final say. The doctors said that there wasn't a risk of J.T. aggravating the injury. The biggest issue was the pain he'd experience.

Mick and I wanted to be ultracautious. But J.T. was not backing down.

"I am finishing this game. I am good to go," he said.

J.T. went the rest of the game. To protect him, we went with a very conservative game plan. The process wasn't pretty. J.T. threw an interception that went for a touchdown on the third offensive play of the second half. Game momentum began to shift in Penn State's favor. He threw another pick on our first possession of the fourth quarter, leading to another score and narrowing our lead to 17–14.

Penn State went on to tie the game with a field goal just before time expired. The game went into overtime and the stadium was reaching a fever pitch. Penn State got the ball and scored a touchdown to start OT. Penn State was keying on Zeke, trying to take away his lanes. J.T. told Tom Herman, our offensive coordinator, that he was ready to carry the ball.

"I'm good, Coach. I'm good. I'm good," he kept saying. Every "good" was louder than the one before. The game was on the line. Zeke took a handoff and went for 3 yards, to the 22. We decided to take J.T. at his word. We called for him to run.

Faking a handoff to Zeke, he kept the ball and ran around the left end, going 17 yards, way down to the Penn State five. We called his number again, a quarterback draw. J.T. ran it in to tie the game.

In the second overtime, an unsportsmanlike conduct penalty by Penn State allowed us to start on the twelve. Zeke ran on first down, but there wasn't much room and he picked up 2 yards. On second down, J.T. dropped back to pass but couldn't find a receiver and took off, this time around the right side, for a 6-yard gain. With the ball on the 4-yard line, we went with the quarterback draw again. J.T. powered for a yard, maybe 2. I was all but certain the play had been stopped, but J.T. never stopped driving, pushing, churning his legs, even though he was wrapped up by multiple defensive players. He got to the 1-yard line, still grinding, and then he lowered his head and got a massive push from behind from guard Pat Elflein.

Somehow, J.T. made it into the end zone. The referee signaled touchdown.

We were ahead by a touchdown. On Penn State's final drive, we stuffed the Penn State running back for no gain. After a 5-yard pass and an incompletion, the game was down to this, a fourth-and-five at our twenty. On the right side of the defensive line, linebacker Josh Perry stood just outside Joey Bosa, our defensive end. When the ball was snapped, Perry rushed up the field, and the offensive tackle peeled outward to make the block. The offensive guard squeezed down onto nose guard Michael Bennett. Unblocked and with a wide lane to the quarterback, Joey charged into the backfield. The running back tried to block him, but Joey drove him backward right into the quarterback, whose legs buckled to the ground from the impact.

The game was over. This hard-fought victory was finally ours.

In the locker room, exhausted and elated, this group of brothers had just faced one of the hardest challenges of the season and prevailed. It was a special moment, especially for defensive line coach Larry Johnson.

For eighteen years, Larry had been the defensive line coach at Penn State and had tremendous success there. We had been fortunate to hire him in January, and now he was on the winning side against the team he'd spent nearly two decades with, watching one of his defensive ends, Joey Bosa, seal the win with a dynamic play. The brotherhood of trust runs beyond just player to player. It is also a bond formed between a coach and his players.

After I said a few words, Coach Mick addressed the team. "You guys have no idea what just happened out there," he said. "For J.T. to do what he did is a testament to who he is and what we are all about. At the end of the game, who made the plays to help win the game?

"He had to make that play. He said, 'I'm not letting my guys down. I AM NOT LETTING MY GUYS DOWN!'"

It was a messy game in many ways. After averaging more than 50 points per game over the previous month, our offense was stagnant during the second half. But we made enough plays to win in a hostile environment. In that locker room, though, the most important thing was that our brotherhood of trust had just grown a little stronger.

We had moved closer to becoming Nine Units Strong.

||||||||||||||||||

Chapter Six: Power of the Unit Playbook

- Unit cohesion is the bond, the deep interpersonal connection, created among the members of the unit.

- Soldiers fight for each other.

- People do not experience your intentions; they experience your behavior.

- Trust is built when people have repeated experience of your behavior in three areas:

  - Character
  - Competence
  - Connection

- The strength of a team is determined by the strength of the connections on the team.

- High levels of performance require deep levels of trust.

- There is no more powerful force than a group of men who share an uncommon commitment to each other and to achieving their mission.

||||||||||||||||||

SEVEN

The Necessity of Alignment

One powerful reason I had a very good feeling about the 2014 team as the season progressed was that our alignment was better than it had been since I arrived at Ohio State.

In order to achieve elite performance, alignment is essential. When a team is aligned, everyone understands and is fully committed to the team's purpose, culture, and strategy. In an aligned organization, every employee—from the executive suite to the loading dock—understands not only the strategies and goals of the business, but also how their individual contribution matters. An aligned organization gets things done faster and with better results and is more agile and responsive to the competitive environment. Alignment is a key ingredient to elite performance because without it the best strategy in the world cannot be executed.

For Ohio State football, all Nine Units must be operating at maximum capacity and must be in alignment. And it starts with the unit leaders.

In physics, the principle of inertia dictates that objects in motion tend to stay in motion unless acted upon by sufficient energy. This principle holds true for objects that are not in motion as well. Objects at rest tend to stay at rest. Inertia also applies to teams. It requires sufficient energy to get a group of players, and a group of units, to align around a common culture in pursuit of a common goal and to execute a common strategy.

That energy is called leadership.

Each player and each unit is moving in a particular direction. The task of a leader is to provide a center of gravity that exerts a pull—attraction and energy—that aligns the trajectory of every player and every unit. In other words, it's leadership that gets every player and every unit on the team going in the same direction.

It's physics.

It's a nonnegotiable law of nature.

For us to be Nine Strong and operate at maximum capacity requires the right amount of leadership energy. It's a balance. On one end of the spectrum, if a leader exerts too much energy, too much gravitational pull, he impairs developmental momentum and slows down his players. These are the command-and-control leaders who try to micromanage everything. They are heavy-handed and harsh in the way they deal with players. Often, they create a culture of fear. As a result, they disconnect, discourage, and demotivate players.

On the other end of the spectrum, when a leader exerts too little energy, too little gravitational pull, the players spin off in all kinds of directions. These are the laissez-faire leaders. They don't demand enough. Their standards are not clear, and they don't hold their players accountable. They are lenient and soft. They want to be buddies or friends with players. They allow an undisciplined culture.

On either end of the spectrum—too controlling or too permissive—you lose alignment, performance suffers, and we are no longer Nine Units Strong.

As I've shared already in this book, we invest heavily in training our unit leaders and our players on how to lead. We don't leave it to chance. In addition to the training sessions we hold, we are constantly talking about leadership. And please understand, these are purposeful conversations that focus on the impact of leadership on our culture and the performance of our team.

Here's how you get alignment:

- Hire the right people and recruit the right players.

- Communicate your purpose and your culture with exceptional clarity and relentless consistency.

- Make it clear to your leaders that it is their responsibility to build and maintain alignment, then equip them with essential skills.

- Hold everyone accountable. If someone is out of alignment, deal with it quickly and decisively.

You'd be surprised how rare it is for teams to be in alignment. In twenty-nine years of coaching, I've been a part of five teams—coaches, players, and support staff—that have been fully aligned. Twenty-four of them were not, and in each instance, the team underperformed because of it. People's lives were affected as well. I learned that lesson as a young man and have never forgotten it.

I was on Earle Bruce's staff at Colorado State for three years, from 1990 through 1992. By the last year, at age twenty-seven, I was making $25,000 per year, with one baby girl already here and Shelley six months pregnant with another. Everything was great until a couple of coaches on Coach Bruce's staff began to undermine him, running to the athletic director, spreading rumors about the program being out of control. It was nasty. And it was wrong. I won't pretend to be neutral on this because Coach Bruce has not just been a life-changing mentor to me, he is a good and honorable man who is practically a second father to me. He did not deserve this—to be betrayed by people to whom he'd given an opportunity. The result was that we were all fired, and I spent two anxious months scrambling to get a job and trying to figure out how I was going to provide for my family.

Ultimately, I was retained by the new coach Colorado State brought in, Sonny Lubick, and then three years later, got hired

With (*left to right*) sister Erika; father, Bud; mother, Gisela; and sister Gigi at the Grotto of Our Lady of Lourdes at Notre Dame. When I was an assistant coach there, it was my favorite place on campus. I visited the grotto every day for four years and said a prayer for my mother when her cancer returned.

Shelley and I present my father with a commemorative piece of the 2006 Florida national championship team.

My father helped make me the man I am. It's an honor to give him a ring after winning the national championship at Florida in 2006.

Shelley and I celebrate a home victory with the traditional singing of the alma mater, "Carmen Ohio."

With my sisters Erika and Gigi and my father.

All three of my children are fine athletes—and all have made
their father proud by being elected captains of their respective teams.

(*Top*) Gigi (No. 5) sets up a Florida Gulf Coast teammate;
(*bottom left*) Nicki competing for the Georgia Tech volleyball team;
(*bottom right*) Nate stretches out to catch a pass for Bishop Watterson High School.

With (*left to right*) Nicki, Shelley, Nate, and Gigi on the annual Buckeye Cruise for Cancer. This event raises more than $1 million for the Urban & Shelley Meyer Fund for Cancer Research.

Visiting the White House is always a huge honor. President Barack Obama welcomes Nate, Shelley, and me a few months after we won the national championship.

With Earle Bruce, my mentor and former OSU coach,
soon after taking the head coaching job at Bowling Green.

Celebrating with my 2004 Utah team moments after beating BYU and finishing the season
11–0 and becoming the "BCS Buster"—the first non-BCS conference team to be invited
to play in a BCS bowl. We went on to beat Pittsburgh in the Fiesta Bowl to wrap up an
undefeated season.

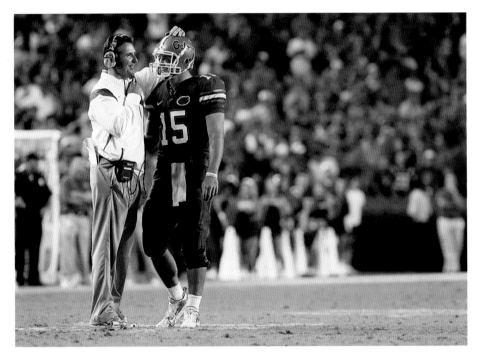

Tim Tebow wasn't just a Heisman Trophy winner.
He was a coach's dream—a guy who always left it all on the field.

Shelley, the kids (*left to right:* Gigi, Nicki, and Nate) and I are introduced
at an Ohio State basketball game not long after I was hired as head coach.

Leading the runout for my first game as head coach at Ohio State, flanked by two of my favorites: team captains John Simon (No. 54) and Zach Boren (No. 44).

Hugging Nate as the final seconds tick off the clock in our 2013 victory over That Team Up North in Ann Arbor.

Leadership consultant Tim Kight leads the team in a Brotherhood of Trust session during the summer of 2014.

Coach Mick leads the team in a pregame tradition known as quick cals.

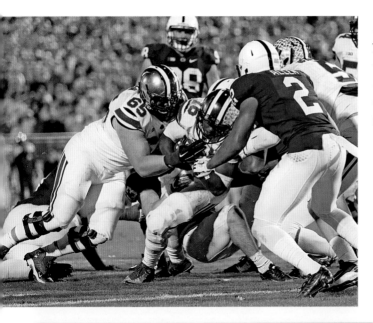

J. T. Barrett scores the winning TD against Penn State in double overtime with the help of a big shove from guard Pat Elflein.

Defensive end Joey Bosa hugs Larry Johnson, our defensive-line coach, after Bosa ended the Penn State game with a walk-off sack. Johnson had been the D-line coach at Penn State for nearly twenty years prior. It was his first time coaching against his former team.

Solitude is critical sometimes. Here I take advantage of some alone time, making final notes before the 2014 Michigan State game.

Safeties coach and co-defensive coordinator Chris Ash runs a drill during pregame with safety Vonn Bell.

Team captains (*left to right*) Doran Grant, Michael Bennett, Curtis Grant, and Jeff Heuerman walk to midfield for the coin toss versus That Team Up North in the final regular season game.

Linebacker Darron Lee returns a fumble caused by Joey Bosa for a touchdown against That Team Up North.

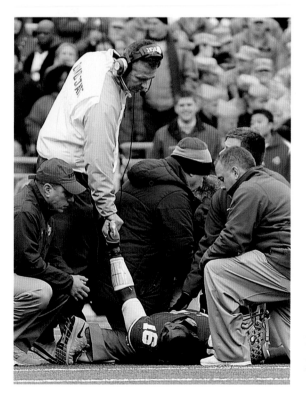

Extending a comforting hand to J. T. Barrett after he broke his ankle against That Team Up North. That's Coach Mick next to J.T. on the left.

Linebacker and team captain Curtis Grant makes a tackle against That Team Up North. Curtis's senior season was a remarkable turnaround.

Wide receiver Devin Smith hauls in one of his three TD passes in the Big Ten championship game.

ABOVE: Defensive tackle Michael Bennett wore No. 53 for the rest of the season following the death of his fellow lineman Kosta Karageorge.

RIGHT: Defensive coordinator Luke Fickell gets a hug after his defense pitched a shutout in the Big Ten championship game against Wisconsin.

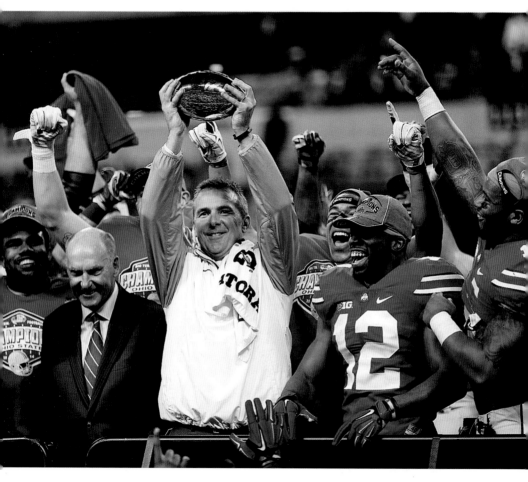

Winning the Big Ten title was a thrill. And best of all, it kept our playoff hopes alive.

A Meyer family hug moments after winning the Big Ten title.

(*Left to right*) Stephen Collier, offensive coordinator and quarterbacks coach Tom Herman, Braxton Miller, J. T. Barrett, and Cardale Jones celebrate after winning the Big Ten championship. Tom and his players did a phenomenal job embracing the Power of the Unit.

Being head coach is a family affair with the team. Gigi and Nicki (*left*) and Nate (*far right*) celebrate the Big Ten championship with the MVP Cardale Jones. Holding up the No. 1 is one of my favorite leaders on the team, No. 68, Taylor Decker.

Here's what the winning locker room looks like after the Big Ten championship game in Lucas Oil Stadium.

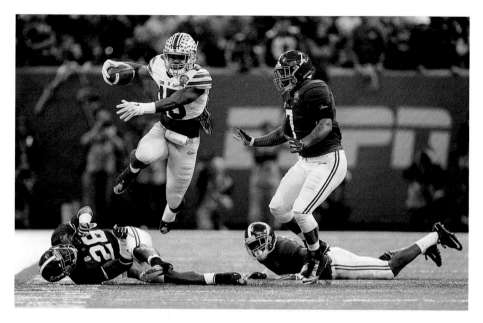

Ezekiel Elliott ran for 230 yards in the Sugar Bowl.
Here he leaps over an Alabama defender for a long gain.

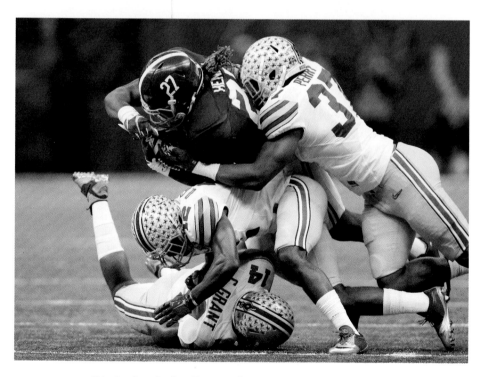

Linebackers Joshua Perry and Curtis Grant and cornerback
Doran Grant make a tackle in the Sugar Bowl.

Team captain and MVP Evan Spencer leaps up to pull down an onside kick in the final minutes of the Sugar Bowl.

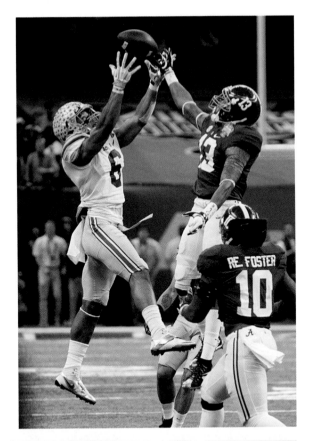

Shelley and I enjoy a moment with the legendary Lou Holtz, one of my greatest mentors, after the Sugar Bowl victory over Alabama.

The Sugar Bowl trophy is pretty heavy. I'm glad Ezekiel Elliott is around to help me lift it.

Quarterback Cardale Jones isn't just big and strong. He can make people miss, as this Oregon defender found out in the national championship game.

With the offensive line and their unit leader, Ed Warinner, during a timeout during the national championship game. Ed's unit was spectacular in our playoff run.

Ezekiel Elliott scores his second of four touchdowns against Oregon in the national championship game. His offensive line played magnificently.

The Ohio State Buckeyes are the first national champions of the College Football Playoff Era.

The wide receivers enjoying the national championship postgame with their unit leader, Zach Smith (in black shirt). Of our 538 yards of offense against Oregon, 242 yards were through the air. (*Left to right*) Cameron Smith (son), Jalin Marshall, Zach Smith, Evan Spencer, Dontre Wilson, Michael Thomas, Jonny Dixon, Devin Smith, Corey Smith.

Kerry Coombs, our cornerbacks and special teams coach, with cornerback Doran Grant after winning the national championship. Kerry was great at building the Power of the Unit not just in his cornerback unit, but within the special teams as well.

Two important members of my leadership cabinet, David Trichel, our director of Post-production, and Tim Kight, our leadership/culture consultant, celebrate on the field after we beat Oregon for the national championship. They are two of my go-to guys.

Our last team/staff shot before we left AT&T Stadium after winning the national title.

by Lou Holtz to join his staff at Notre Dame, a dream job for a football-loving Catholic, but I've never forgotten the wreckage that was caused at Colorado State because the staff wasn't in alignment and because of the disloyalty I witnessed. To this day, I regret that I didn't do more to stop it. I love Earle Bruce, and yet I didn't have the courage to confront these guys.

I'm so committed to never going through anything like that again that all these years later, I have a conversation with my coaches and their spouses before every season, and let them know that to me disloyalty is insubordination, and if you are insubordinate you are gone. It's not "Oops, sorry, I didn't mean anything by it." It's "Pack your bags and get out of here."

I don't have any hard data to back this up, but I'd guess that alignment problems result in many more lost football games than any shortage of talent does. Leading up to the 2014 season, I asked my unit leaders how many times they have ever been on a staff that was fully aligned, a team with Nine Units Strong.

They all replied, "None."

I got an unwanted reminder of that once when I hired two offensive assistants who didn't really believe in what we were doing with the spread offense. Don't get me wrong: they were knowledgeable coaches with impressive résumés. I fault me for hiring them because even though they were good football guys, they were not a good fit for our system. I allowed myself to be so caught up with where they'd been and what they'd done that I didn't listen to my own instincts.

Week after week, these guys wanted to inject things into

our system that wouldn't fit. They would lobby to put in concepts that were too complex and didn't have any carryover or relationship to our system.

It was a constant headache for me. The low point happened when we were preparing for a rivalry game and a chance to defend an undefeated regular season. I was walking out to practice with my one of my offensive players on Wednesday before the game.

He looked at me as we were walking.

"You know, if we put in this play I think it would make things better," he said.

"What did you say?"

"I think this play would work against that defense."

We were about to practice and I didn't want to get into a big thing with him, but all I could think was, "Wow, we have a major alignment problem here. Instead of talking about our offense in the meeting room, they're filling his head and talking about what they want to do and not what we're going to do."

Usually I let my coaches go home after Wednesday practices to get some family time, but not this week. We all went upstairs for about three hours and put together the game plan. We won the game easily, but the pain from the headache didn't go away the whole year.

I wound up spending hours and hours each week in the offensive meeting rooms making sure they weren't straying from our core offensive system, and leaving me with serious concerns about how our offense was going to perform on Saturday.

How could I not be concerned, when the coaches most closely involved didn't believe in it? How much genuine enthusiasm is there going to be in the teaching? All the time I spent dealing with this was time I couldn't spend keeping an eye on the bigger picture and leading my team.

Bill Belichick has often told me, "Always bring in people who can enhance what you do without changing the basics of it." Sometimes, of course, you need to blow something up and start over, the way we did with our secondary in 2014, but that wasn't the case here. We were looking for enhancement while remaining true to our core. That's the point I want to underscore. Bring in people who believe in what you are doing and will help you make it better.

The perfect example was when we hired Tom Herman from Iowa State as offensive coordinator and quarterbacks coach. Tom wasn't the biggest name out there, and if the media and OSU fans knew about the people who wanted that job, they probably would've told me I'd lost my mind. But Tom did some great things at Iowa State, plus he's got a ton of expertise in the up-tempo offense. Right away, I could tell how smart and charismatic he was. During the interview I handed him our playbook.

"Study this. I'll be back in one hour. Teach it to me," I told him.

When I returned, he basically taught me the whole offense.

Being challenged is great. I challenge our players and staff on a daily basis, and I want them to challenge me if they think something can be improved. One of the core messages I hope you take away from this book is that the constant pursuit of knowledge and improvement, striving to make yourself better today than you were yesterday, is not merely an indispensable tenet for leaders to follow, but one of the great joys of life. It is a pursuit that motivates me every day to be a better husband, a better father, a better Christian, a better friend, and a better football coach.

The lessons learned have made me more vigilant than ever about the people who are around me. I've had some phenomenal assistants over the years, but I have to say that the 2014 staff at Ohio State—coaches and support personnel—was one of the best. They are profoundly loyal and passionate about getting to Nine Units Strong. They are skilled and dedicated teachers who embrace our core values and work their tails off to be the best. Even as I wrote this chapter, Brian Voltolini, our director of operations, was visiting Champaign, Illinois, Indianapolis, and Oklahoma City to scout out hotel options for the 2016 season. There are specific things we look for in a hotel—meeting-room space, privacy, and menu planning are three of the main concerns—and Brian wanted to do all the reconnaissance himself. In fact, he wouldn't have it any other way. Overkill? Some might say that, but I don't like surprises. In football and every other business, so many small things go into a smooth operation, and all of those small things contribute to your alignment. When we have a road game, the operational details that Brian manages would boggle your mind. He coordinates with the OSU travel department to plan departure details and food service en route. We have to give the charter company information on our gross weight (players and cargo) and have a seating plan on board to make sure the weight is evenly distributed. (The starting offensive and defensive linemen get first class; they need the extra room). We have police escorts for our buses on every leg of the trip, both in Columbus and wherever we are going. Amy Nicol, my assistant, flies a day ahead of time to make sure everything is squared away in the hotel we're traveling to, from the menus to the meeting rooms where we do our walk-throughs.

Not long ago I was recruiting a blue-chip player who was coveted by just about everybody, but in the course of conducting our due diligence, I learned some things that called into question his practice habits as well as some of his off-the-field decision-making. I like gifted players as much as the next coach, but I had enough doubts about how hard this kid would be willing to work and how committed he would be to our core beliefs that I decided to back off.

This is not an exact science, by any means. Some kids go through rough patches and then mature a little later. Others have rough patches that wind up lasting their entire lives. As I've gone through my own maturation process as a coach and leader, I've tried to become more and more judicious about seeking out only those kids I think will have the best chance to stay aligned with what we teach and how we train.

Otherwise, you run the risk of not only wasting a scholarship, but setting yourself up for four years of headaches that you don't need.

C oaching legend Nick Aliotti confirmed for me the power of alignment. I've known Nick for close to twenty-five years, most of which he has spent as the defensive coordinator for the University of Oregon. When I took my leave from coaching and toured programs around the country, Oregon was one of my stops. I was at one of Chip Kelly's practices, standing with Nick, a very successful and well-respected coach who is as old school as you can get—just a rough, tough throwback football coach. Chip had music from *The Lion King* blaring the morning I was there. He had a DJ at practice. I have never played music at practice, ever. That is not the message I want to send. We're not there to listen to music. We're there to play football and get better.

I mentioned something along those lines to Nick, and he stopped me.

"You know what, Urban? This is the only way to do it," he said.

I couldn't believe what I'd just heard. I must've misunderstood. I asked Nick to repeat himself.

"It's the *only* way to do it," he said again.

I knew right then why Chip Kelly was so successful. It was not this space-age offense. It wasn't the color of the uniforms or even the music he played at practice. It was his uncanny gift for making everybody around him believe that what he's doing is the best—for getting everybody totally buying in and aligned. I mean, he had Nick Aliotti, Mr. Old School, sold on blasting music at practice. There's not a chance in the world that Nick thought this was the only way to do it five years earlier. Chip convinced him that it was. I left there with my respect for the importance of alignment affirmed.

||||||||||||||||

Chapter Seven: The Necessity of Alignment Playbook

- In order to achieve elite performance, alignment is essential.

- An aligned organization gets things done faster and with better results, and is more agile and responsive to the competitive environment.

- Achieving alignment requires effective leadership. Avoid the extremes of command and control and leniency. Find the balance.

- Bring in people who believe in what you are doing and will help you make it better.

- Hold everyone accountable. If someone is out of alignment, deal with it quickly and decisively.

||||||||||||||||

||||||||||||||||||||||||||||||

EIGHT

The 10-80-10 Principle

HOW TO BUILD AN ELITE TEAM

There is a theory about human behavior called the 10-80-10 principle. I speak of it often when I talk to corporate groups or business leaders. It is the best strategy I know for getting the most out of your team. Think of your team or your organization as a big circle. At the very center of it, the nucleus, are the top 10 percenters, people who give all they've got all the time, who are the essence of self-discipline, self-respect, and the relentless pursuit of improvement.

They are the elite—the most powerful component of any organization.

They are the people I love to coach.

Outside the nucleus are the 80 percenters. They are the majority—people who go to work, do a good job, and are relatively reliable. The 80 percenters are for the most part trustworthy and dutiful, but they simply don't have the drive and the unbending will that the nucleus guys do. They just don't burn as hot.

The final 10 percenters are uninterested or defiant. They are on the periphery, mostly just coasting through life, not caring about reaching their potential or honoring the gifts they've been given. They are coach killers.

The leadership challenge is to move as many of the 80 percenters into the nucleus as you can. If you can expand the top 10 percent into 15 percent or 20 percent, you are going to see a measurable increase in the performance of your team. By the end of the 2014 season, our nucleus group was close to 30 percent. We did that by challenging our top 10 percent to identify and go get some of the 80 percenters and, in turn, influence the 80 percent to elevate their level of play, deepen their commitment, and give more of themselves for the program. We wanted our top 10 percent to be leaders who influenced and motivated others. This is essential because leadership is about connecting. Leadership is an activity that happens person to person and heart to heart. It's about engaging deeply with others and inspiring them to be better.

When I coached Tim Tebow at Florida, he was a leader and an influencer. He'd come in my office and we'd say to each other, "Let's go get an eighty today and get him into the top ten." It was a daily, intentional priority for Tim and for me.

How well you perform as a team is going to depend on the work you do with the 80 percenters. That's why I devote more time to them by far than to either of the 10 percenters. As much as you love your top 10 percenters, you don't need to motivate them because they are doing it by themselves. Everybody—coaches, staff, trainers—wants to be around these elite people. They are positive, high-achieving people, and it's fun to associate with them. But remember, your goal as a leader is to build and motivate your whole team, and the way to do that is to focus your attention on the 80 percenters.

On the other end, the bottom 10 percenters are not really worth wasting any energy on. It took me a while to realize this. For years I would try to change them. I would look at their corner-cutting ways and take it as a challenge to make them see the virtue and satisfaction that comes with working hard and getting results. It was probably arrogant on my part to think I could get them to change. The lesson I learned was this: time is a nonrenewable resource. If you waste it, you never get it back, so it's essential to pick your battles wisely.

We talk about that at length at Ohio State. The hours you spend trying to motivate a guy who doesn't care about getting better or about being there for the team are hours you would be much better off investing elsewhere. Players under stress from problematic family situations or dealing with drug-related issues, my staff and I will do whatever we can to help. If you want to get better and battle through adversity, we will be right there with you. The bottom 10 percent that I'm referring to are the players who have only one gear and don't want to find another one. I had a player once who was the quintessential bottom 10 percent guy. He had the natural ability not only to make it to the NFL, but to be a really good NFL player. He was smart and had many advantages to capitalize on. He was on scholarship for four years, but the money that the school spent on him was wasted. He did little as a player and even less as a student. I talked to him. Mentored him. Other coaches did as well. We tried to help him see how he was slacking his way right out of a degree. Our efforts proved futile.

When we discover that a player is willfully resistant to our efforts and refuses to take advantage of the resources we provide, we redirect our attention elsewhere. Kobe Bryant expressed it well. "I can't relate to lazy people," he said. "We don't speak the same language. I don't understand you. I don't want to understand you."

I am going to lay out specific ways of moving the 80 percenters into the high-performing group, but before I do let's look at the bigger picture of the 10-80-10 principle and the whole concept of talent.

I like having talented players as much as the next coach. That said, I think that we tend to overrate the importance of talent. I think we, as a nation, are obsessed with it. We want to believe that having talent guarantees greatness. We want to believe we can accurately gauge somebody's greatness with times, measurements, and data. What's your IQ? What's your forty time? Your vertical leap? Your fastball reading on the radar gun? Your SAT score? Your bench press? Give me your numbers, and I will tell you how good you are, and how good you can be.

But statistics don't play the game.

Football leads the charge in all of this. Look at the endless reports we get from the NFL combine. Look at the lists spit out by all those recruiting service rankings, telling us that this guy is five stars and that guy is four stars, as if it were the final word.

Except that's not how the real world works. The number of stars next to a guy's name or where a school might rate on someone's list of the best recruiting classes is nothing but a highly subjective snapshot. Maybe it will turn out to be accurate. Or maybe it won't. There are even multiple Web sites that actually declare a national recruiting championship. I understand this is all driven by the huge fan following that college football has. The point is that a pile of numbers is not nearly as important as how hard a guy works and how driven he is to get better.

Mariano Rivera, the greatest relief pitcher of all time, signed with the Yankees for $2,000 and a glove and was not even in the top fifty prospects in rookie ball when he started. Aaron Rodgers went to a junior college because nobody thought he was a Division I quarterback, and he only wound up at Cal-Berkeley because the coach saw him when he was recruiting somebody else. Malcolm Butler, Super Bowl hero, was unrated out of high school, played at the University of West Alabama, and was picked up as an unrestricted free agent by the New England Patriots.

Not a single starter for either team in Super Bowl XLIX

was rated a five-star recruit out of high school. Think about that. I have learned that being elite is not about how talented you are; it's about how tough and committed you are to getting better.

Of the many players I've coached, John Simon, former OSU captain and now linebacker with the Houston Texans, was one of the most dedicated athletes I've ever seen. Early in his senior year—my first year in Columbus—Simon played a game against Cal-Berkeley with basically one shoulder. John was in a great deal of pain and made key plays in our 35–28 victory. After the game he gave a locker room speech that I'll never forget. It was one of the most moving moments I've ever had as a coach. With great emotion, John opened up, gave us his heart, and challenged every one of us—coaching staff included—to look at what we were giving and how much we cared. I was so blown away that afterward I told the media I would name our next child after him. (OK, so I got a little carried away.) With someone like John Simon, you never have to say a word to motivate him or get him to push himself. I would put our current guys like Joshua Perry and Taylor Decker in the same category. Both of them are top 10 percenters. They are elite performers for our team and high achievers in the classroom. They do the right things and push the guys around them, the 80 percenters, to become better. They are the ultimate competitors.

Here are four approaches to getting as many of your 80 percenters as possible into the inner circle:

Mastery and Belief

If players are going to make the big push to join the elites, they need to believe it will be worth it. It's important to remind them of the quality of the leadership at Ohio State—let them know they are being taught by masters of their craft who have made a significant difference in other players' lives. I make sure that my assistant coaches showcase the achievements of other great players they have worked with. Visuals such as videos and images are incredible tools to convey a message. When a player walks into Luke Fickell's office, I want him to see photos of Ohio State greats A. J. Hawk, James Laurinaitis, and Ryan Shazier, all of whom Luke has coached. When a player walks into the office of Ed Warinner, our offensive coordinator, I want him to see Warinner's three former OSU offensive lineman who started as rookies in the NFL—Corey Linsley, Jack Mewhort, and Andrew Norwell. It may not seem like a big deal, but these sorts of associations are important. It is not about bragging. It's about reinforcing that this is a special place that has produced special players. It's about motivating the 80 percenters.

When I walk in my own office and I see championship trophies, photos with presidents, keepsakes, and mementos and clippings of the Heisman Trophy finalists and winners I've coached, I feel good. If a prospective recruit is motivated by wanting to be part of that club, well, that makes me feel good, too.

It's a natural human reaction to want to be connected to

greatness. The moment you arrive in the lobby of our football complex, you see trophies, photos, and multimedia displays of some of the great moments in Ohio State history, dating to the first national championship in 1942. Walk through the double doors and down the main hallway, and the length of it features such Ohio State football legends as Archie Griffin, Eddie George, Orlando Pace, and Chris Spielman. This isn't theory. It's testimony. This is who played here. This is what they achieved. Who wouldn't want to be a part of this great tradition? The underlying message is: "This could be you. All you need to do is work, train, and live Above the Line. Be as fully committed to getting better as the guys whose pictures you are looking at."

Harness the Power

The top 10 percenters, as we've noted, are the greatest asset your organization has—the elite achievers. These are the John Simons you want out there in the fourth quarter of a big game, or the Joshua Perrys and Taylor Deckers, who set an example by performing at the highest of their abilities. So we aim to leverage the influence and credibility of the top 10 percent to maximum advantage.

As a young coach, I savored every second I could be around Earle Bruce and Lou Holtz. I wanted to absorb everything I could possibly learn from these great men. Players such as Simon have similar drawing power, and I'm sure it's no different with guys like LeBron James, Mike Trout, and Sidney Crosby. Elite performers in businesses and other organizations have this same effect.

Left unchecked, most people will keep the company of like-minded people. In other words, the top 10 percenters will stick with their fellow 10 percenters, and the 80 percenters will do the same with their group. We work hard to change that inclination, pairing a top 10 percenter with an 80 percenter as much as possible in workouts, drills, and unit meetings. Harness the power that the elites have. Leverage the ability of the top 10 percenters to bring more 80 percenters into the nucleus.

When Simon was captain and leader of the undefeated 2012 team, he would come to the weight room by himself every day at 6 A.M. to train. One day I pulled him aside.

"You can't come in to lift at 6 A.M. anymore," I said.

He looked at me, puzzled.

"You know that I love your work ethic," I said. "This is about using you as a magnet—getting more players to go about their work the way you do. You can keep coming in, of course, but there's one rule: you have to bring somebody with you." He did, and it had a significant impact. It's been such a success that Coach Mick won't let the top 10 percenters in the weight room if they don't bring along an 80 percenter.

David Nelson was a wide receiver for me at Florida, a fine young man with a lot of talent who was another quintessential 80 percenter. Tebow and I and others on the staff had been working to get him into the inner circle for the better part of three years, but it just wasn't happening. When I got to my office the morning after we lost to Ole Miss in 2008, our only defeat of the season, David Nelson was sitting outside. He was in tears.

"I want to make an impact on this team. I want to make a difference," he said. He told me he felt ashamed that he'd wasted his first three years by not pushing himself hard all the time, the way Tebow did. Now he wanted to do all he could to change that.

"You can make a huge impact, David," I said. "You can start today. It starts with your heart and how much you want this. The more you are willing to give of yourself, the more you are going to get."

From that day forward, David Nelson became a top 10 percenter. He gave relentless effort every day. The change in him was remarkable. After Percy Harvin was injured in the SEC Championship game, David Nelson caught a touchdown pass that gave us the lead. In the BCS National Championship game, he scored the game-winning touchdown, grabbing a jump pass from Tebow.

I can't think of a better example of harnessing the power of the 10 percent.

Building Ownership

When a player or employee feels an ownership stake in what's going on, he gives maximum effort. As a young coach at Illinois State in the town of Normal, Illinois, I rented my first apartment. It was a shabby place with a leaky toilet, scuffed-up walls, and cabinets that looked as if they might not stay on the walls. One night, I had some friends over to watch the heavyweight fight between Mike Tyson and Buster Douglas. When Douglas won in a shocking knockout, one of my friends jumped off the couch and kicked a hole in the wall. In the time-honored tradition of young and penniless renters everywhere, I moved the couch to hide the damage.

A couple of years later, when I joined Earle Bruce's staff at Colorado State, Shelley and I saved up and bought our first house, for a whopping $75,000. If the same guy kicked a hole in one of our new walls, I would've made absolutely sure he fixed it as soon as possible. It's different when you are invested and have something at stake.

So I started to give the 80 percenter guys more and more ownership. We have a ring committee that designs the jewelry when we win a championship, and I select guys to design the rings. When we have to make a decision about jersey styles and colors, I select guys to get involved in that also. It's the same with locker room décor, and some of the menu options at training table. The more ways your people can share ownership, the more loyal and committed they are going to be.

Positive Peer Pressure

On the east end of our indoor training facility, there's a section we call The Grind. It is the place where players can put in extra work honing their football skills. The top 10 percenters practically live there. The receivers go there to catch footballs and tennis balls fired from a JUGS machine. Defensive backs go to fine-tune their footwork, and offensive linemen work hand placement on dummies.

The Grind is headquarters for extra effort, the after-hours spot of the elite. It is where athletes go when they've moved beyond all excuse making or resistance. It is where champions are made. We have large wall banners of some of our greatest players above the area as both a tribute and motivation. One of the forces that gets our 80 percenters to move up is the culture they are immersed in. Everybody is pushing each other to get better. They are pushing hard. We cannot afford to settle into complacency. If you are going through the motions, staying in the same place, there's a good chance somebody is going to move right past you. This isn't something we use as an overt threat, but the message is clear. The world is a competitive place. To compete at an elite level, you need to train at an elite level.

If you are seeing this in your organization, enhance it and keep going. If not, lead the change that will make it a priority. Remember that the real power of your leadership is not your level of authority, but your level of influence. Your chances of ordering an 80 percenter into the top 10 percent are negligible. But your chances of influencing the shift by using the strategies we've discussed are excellent. Harness the power of your elite performers. Greatness happens when you are able to maximize their impact on the 80 percenters.

Tim Tebow reminded me just how profound this dynamic can be, after that Ole Miss defeat that David Nelson was so torn up about. At the end of his postgame press conference, Tim became emotional. He had to stop and compose himself. He felt that he hadn't performed up to his own expectations or his team's expectations.

He closed by saying this:

I'm sorry. Extremely sorry. We were hoping for an undefeated season. That was my goal—something Florida has never done here. But I promise you one thing. A lot of good will come out of this. You will never see any player in the entire country play as hard as I will play the rest of the season and you will never see someone push the rest of the team as hard as I will push everybody the rest of the season, and you will never see any team play harder than we will the rest of the season.

God Bless.

And then he left the podium.

We didn't lose a game the rest of the season.

Michael Thomas, our talented wide receiver, is a good example of someone who moved from being an 80 percenter to the top 10 percent. Michael has tremendous gifts, but his transition to college football wasn't easy. He was a good worker and did fine academically. But there was an arrogance in his attitude that prevented him from buying in to our culture.

He played sparingly as a freshman, then struggled early in his sophomore season. Talent wasn't the issue, but mistakes and accountability were. Every third play it seemed that he'd run the wrong route or make the wrong read and he'd always have an excuse for it. I got tired of the excuses and decided he needed a year to work on his game, learn to be accountable, and grow up. So we red-shirted him, which is rare for a second year player without an injury. It was a jarring change for him to have to sit out a whole season. I challenged him—very much on purpose.

Following the 2013 season, I called a meeting with Michael and his dad. We discussed what Michael needed to do in order to fix the problem areas in both his technique and his attitude. "You can be one of the best receivers in the country," I told him. "It's up to you. I know you have big dreams. I want to help you fulfill them. But if your habits don't reflect your dreams and goals, you can either change your habits or change your dreams and goals."

And Michael took the message to heart.

He absorbed what was said and changed his work habits. He enlisted the help of Evan Spencer and the two began training together often. As a result, Michael's technical skill as a wide receiver grew and along the way he became a better brother to his unit.

If your habits are not in alignment with your dreams you can either lower your dreams or elevate your habits. Michael Thomas elevated.

When I was at Florida, we had a kid named Cornelius Ingram, a small-town quarterback who was six feet four inches and 225 pounds and was widely billed as the second coming of Texas's Vince Young. Certainly everybody in Hawthorne, the tiny north-central Florida community he was born and raised in, thought he was the next Vince Young. Cornelius was recruited by schools all over the country, and he chose Florida; he was such a gifted athlete that he played for coach Billy Donovan's Florida basketball team, too. I inherited Ingram when I took over in 2005, and the more I got a feel for our personnel, the more convinced I was that Cornelius's future was as a tight end. We had Chris Leak at quarterback, and freshman Tim Tebow right behind him. Cornelius was big and strong and had great hands, and my football instincts told me that tight end would be a better fit.

The trouble was that Cornelius wanted no part of it. When I first broached the idea of a position switch to him, he looked at me as if I were joking.

"Coach, I'm a quarterback. I was recruited as a quarterback. I've always been a quarterback," he said.

"I understand that, Cornelius, but you have everything you need to be an outstanding tight end. You would have an immediate impact there, and I'm not sure we can say that at quarterback with the people we have. I think it's worth exploring."

Cornelius had trouble breaking into Billy's rotation in basketball, and now I was stomping on his quarterback dream. There were plenty of schools that were ready to let him play quarterback.

We definitely did not want to lose him. Steve Addazio, then the tight ends coach, and I worked hard to urge him to think this through carefully and understand that just because some other school may hand him the ball to play quarterback doesn't mean that it would be in his best interests to do that. Cornelius finally agreed to give tight end a go during spring practice of 2006, and I knew that right away this needed to go well.

We had to create success for him. Find small victories to stoke his enthusiasm, and get this transition off to a good start.

In those first scrimmages that spring, Cornelius was going against man-to-man coverage almost exclusively. He was catching a lot of balls. We told him we'd use him in different ways, sometimes lining him behind center as a wildcat quarterback. He liked that idea. We called his wildcat number one day near the end of a practice that he'd dominated. I looked over at Charlie Strong, then our co–defensive coordinator, to make sure we were in a coverage that would help the play work.

Cornelius took the snap, pitched the ball to the tailback, and went out for a pass. He sprinted out into the flat, the tailback threw a good ball, and Cornelius Ingram, one-time quarterback now warming up nicely to tight end, took it to the end zone. It was the start of a great run by Cornelius, who was a key part of our victory to capture the 2006 National Championship. He went on to be drafted by the Philadelphia Eagles and sign a contract for almost $2 million.

Obviously, there are limits to how often you can script success this way on the football field. However, nothing encourages an athlete more than making plays and having success in practice. Small victories can play a major role when you have a player who is dealing with the stress of change or even some other issue. Do whatever you can to reinforce someone's confidence by helping him achieve small victories. So much of leadership comes down to knowing the people you are leading and providing them with what they need to succeed. It is also about making them confident to take risks and make changes.

"Failure is not fatal," John Wooden said, "but a failure to change might be."

When I think about having the courage to change, I think about Marty Johnson. Marty, a tailback for me at the University of Utah, had come from a difficult background in Sacramento but had a world of potential. Marty was leading the nation in rushing a couple of weeks into the 2002 season, a year before I arrived, until a severe knee injury ended the season for him. Dealing with the sting of not being on the field, he started making a string of Below the Line decisions. The culmination of those decisions led to him getting busted for a DUI. He was given a suspended jail sentence and probation.

I met with him when I was hired in 2003. A young man with little family structure and a long way from home, Marty struck me as an at-risk player but also a terrific, earnest guy who wanted to do the right thing. I had great faith in his basic goodness. My wife, Shelley, is a psychiatric nurse with a specialty in addiction. She felt the same way about Marty as I did. We started inviting him over to our house for dinner. He befriended our daughter Gigi and became a regular at Gigi's baseball games. Everything was going well. With positive momentum in his life, Marty seemed to be in a much better place. Then early one morning, I received a phone call that he'd been arrested on a second DUI charge, about a year after his first one. I felt angry and betrayed. My initial response was that I was done with him. I hoped he'd go to jail for a long time. He had his chance, and he blew it.

When I got to the office, I passed by a stack of newspapers and saw a horrific headline about a little girl being killed by a drunk driver. The driver wasn't Marty Johnson, and the story had nothing to do with him, but the thought of what this family must be going through just ripped me up. That could've been one of our daughters. Marty's arrest was a huge story in Salt Lake City, a place that does not take kindly to this sort of transgression. We were all set to dismiss him from the team and from school, but then I had a long talk with Shelley and we decided that we wanted to push to give Marty another chance. Maybe he'd get it. Maybe he'd change and not be the guy in a tragic headline the next time. Shelley knows better than anyone how pernicious addictions can be and how easy it is to relapse. It doesn't mean you coddle people and say, "Oh, he didn't mean it. He's a good person." It means that if you truly believe someone wants to get sober and wants to make good decisions, you give him another chance. It has nothing do with winning football games. It has to do with saving a life. The easy thing would've been to dismiss him. It takes much more time and energy and patience to help a kid make meaningful changes.

I knew we'd get blistered in the media if we kept him. "I don't care what the media says," Shelley said. "They can write and say whatever they want. We are talking about somebody's life."

I suspended Marty for the whole season, and we set specific ground rules for him to adhere to in order for him to return to the team. He had to abide by a curfew, go through counseling, and submit to random drug and alcohol tests. On Thanksgiving Day 2003, Marty Johnson went to jail for a month-long sentence as a consequence for the second DUI. Gigi and I went to visit him, and when he came out in his prison-issue orange jumpsuit, I about lost it. We sat down behind a safety-glass partition and talked to him. Gigi reached her hand through the bottom and held Marty's hand.

"Why did you do that?" she asked him.

Marty started to cry. We all shed tears that day.

Upon his release, we kept Marty close to our family, supporting his sobriety and his return to the university. During his senior season, Marty was a significant contributor to our undefeated 2004 team and accounted for 848 yards of total offense and fifteen touchdowns.

"If the Meyers had given up on me," Marty said, "I don't know where I'd be."

It's never easy to read people's capacity for change. After watching Marty reclaim his life, I am much more willing to give players a second and even a third chance to turn things around. My wife and kids would be in tears oftentimes when they would hear stories about players going through unimaginable personal difficulties, and it used to rip me up to see how much it was hurting them. I'm better at it now because of the testimony I've seen from players who had the courage to fix the problem areas in their life and change. Giving up on somebody takes nothing. Helping them change takes a tremendous amount of time, energy, discipline, and love.

In the end, it's worth it.

There are some situations that don't end so fortunately. There are some that are so tragic, they leave permanent scars.

Avery Atkins was one of our top recruits at Florida, a dynamic athlete and charismatic guy from a rough neighborhood in Daytona. He was a great player who had first-round NFL talent in him, and also, he was my kids' favorite player. They would frequently ask about how he was doing and when they were going to get to see him again.

Avery started a few games for us as a true freshman and showed great promise going into his sophomore year. He became a father early in his college career, but after getting arrested for a misdemeanor domestic battery charge, I had to remove him from the team. He transferred to a Division 1-AA school to continue his career. After three games with his new team, he abruptly left, moved back to Daytona, and got involved with drugs. It broke my heart when I heard about this. My assistant coach, Chuck Heater, now the defensive coordinator at Marshall University, loved Avery like a son. Aside from being a great football coach, Chuck is as big-hearted a man as you will find. During a bye week on his own accord, he went up to Daytona to look for Avery. When he found him, Avery was high on something. Avery had a very strong support group with his mom, aunt, and grandmother, all of whom are wonderful people. Chuck met with them, and afterward talked to me about finding a way to get Avery back. "We've got to give him one more chance," I said. "Let's see if we can get him back here and help him."

I went to the college president and the athletic director and stated our case to do all we could to help this young man. They were reluctant, but they trusted me. "We'll make him walk on," I said. "We'll make him earn his scholarship. This is a kid crying out for help, and I believe we need to help him."

They agreed and Avery was readmitted to the University of Florida, paying his own way. He, Coach Heater, and I had a long talk when he got back on campus and he seemed very grateful for the opportunity. It was January, the beginning of the spring term in 2007. Classes had just started. I was going out for a run when I saw Avery pull up in his car right outside my office. One thing I've learned over the years is that you can tell a lot about a kid by opening his car door. If it's a mess—I mean, an out-of-control mess, with empty cans and McDonald's bags and dirty laundry—it typically means other things might be out of control also.

Avery's car was a mess, and so was Avery.

"Let's go for a ride," I said.

He started to drive and tears began to stream down his face. He talked about the pressures he was feeling, about all these things going on with the baby and his girlfriend. You could tell it was as if his world were caving in on him. He just needed to talk.

He drove and we talked. About a half-hour later, we were back outside my office. "You're going to be all right, Avery," I said. "Come by my office tomorrow. We'll talk some more. It's going to be OK."

"Thanks, Coach," Avery said. "I appreciate all you and Coach Heater are doing for me."

It was the last time I ever saw Avery Atkins.

He dropped out of school and went back to Daytona, the streets, and the drugs. Five months later, I received a phone call. Avery Atkins had died of a drug overdose in his car. He was twenty years old.

For years, Avery Atkins's death haunted me, a horrific tape playing on endless loop in my head: *This was on my watch. How could this happen? What should I have done?* I used to talk about it with Tebow, Shelley, and those closest to me, all the time. I prayed about it, asking for clarity. It was one of those instances when you know that God has a plan, but you have a difficult time understanding what it might be.

The deeper we went into the 2014 season, I could sense that more and more 80 percent guys were pushing into the top 10 percenters. Evan Spencer, our senior wide receiver and a top 10 percent guy to his core, was not just one of our MVPs and one of our top leaders. He was a player who completely embraced the idea of harnessing the power of the elite among the receivers unit.

"I did everything in my power to bring people with me,"

Evan said. "I worked my tail off, but that wasn't enough. I wanted the other guys to work their tails off too, and did all I could to lead by example by going out there and taking care of business every day."

In words and actions, I wanted to get the point across that we were on the cusp of something great, and we had do everything in our power to get better every day. Not just some of us—all of us. This was the mindset of our program.

The offensive line was getting better protecting J.T., and on the defensive side of the ball, players like linebacker Curtis Grant and tackle Michael Bennett, both seniors, were suddenly playing with enormous energy and effectiveness. We were controlling the line of scrimmage on both sides of the ball, getting big-time performances from a number of our 80 percenters. The top 10 percent, our nucleus, was growing every day. Game by game, they were showing me their potential to be exceptional.

I liked what I was seeing.

||||||||||||||||||

Chapter Eight: The 10-80-10 Principle Playbook

- Every team or organization consists of three groups:

  - The top 10 percent: disciplined, driven, self-motivated, want to be great, and work relentlessly.
  - The 80 percent: the majority—those who do a good job and are relatively reliable.
  - The bottom 10 percent: disinterested and defiant.

- The key to success is moving as many of the 80 percenters into the top 10 percent as you can.

- Time is a limited resource. Stop wasting it trying to motivate the bottom 10 percent.

- Here are four approaches to move the 80 percenters into the top 10 percent:

  - Mastery and belief: remind them of the quality of leadership; let them know they are being taught by masters of their craft.
  - Harness the power of the elite: everybody wants to be around the top 10 percenters. Use them to motivate the 80 percenters.

- Ownership: the more sense of ownership you can instill in your people, the more motivated they will be to push into the top 10 percent.
- Positive peer pressure: everybody is pushing each other to get better.

|||||||||||||||||||

|||||||||||||||||||||||||||||||||||||

NINE

Think Like
a Leader

"A public opinion poll is no substitute for thought."
—WARREN BUFFETT

Every great leader I have been around or studied has demonstrated the unique ability to think. To think deeply, originally, and often, bravely. Leadership is a mindset first and a skill set second. If you don't think like a leader, you won't act like one.

I invited Dan Gilbert, founder of Quicken Loans and owner of the Cleveland Cavaliers, to speak to our team. One of the many lessons I learned from him that day was, "Thinking about problems, challenges, new ways of doing things and creativity is one of *the* hardest things you will ever do. It also brings you the finest results."

I put a high priority on thinking. I'm a guy whose wheels rarely stop turning. An insight or breakthrough idea can come to you at any time, and you have to be ready. I keep a notepad by my bed so that when an idea pops into my head, I won't forget it after a night of sleep. I write notes on my phone when I'm walking on a treadmill. When I am driving, I often turn the radio off because the quiet helps me concentrate.

I did as much thinking in the early months of 2014 as I have at any time in my coaching career. I thought for hours about how and why the previous season had ended with those defeats, and what we could do to address the reasons for them. And those solitary, thoughtful moments gave me the awareness to understand what we needed to do, from teaching our purpose with exceptional clarity, to building the brotherhood of trust, to making sure we were completely aligned with helping our players get and stay Above the Line.

When things aren't going right, the most important thing you can do is slow down, go deep, and figure out why. It is very easy in the world we live in to get so caught up in the tyranny of the urgent that we don't make time to think. There are many distractions that pull leaders away from investing the time necessary to reflect on the issues and challenges facing their organizations.

Dan Gilbert is right: it is very hard to do.

But there is an even bigger issue here. A lot of people really don't want to think deeply. They'd prefer to play it safe, not rock the boat, and never stray far from the status quo. I've met a lot of people in my life who went to good schools, got good grades, and generally do good work but have minimal ability to think on their feet.

|||||||||||||||||||

Sometimes I wonder if we've graduated an entire generation of hoop jumpers in America. You say the rule, they
comply. You name the standard, they comply. You pick the task,
they comply. But when you ask them to give you an original
thought, listen to the silence. There's so much emphasis these
days on test scores and class rank that I think we're not doing
enough to find the problem solvers and the truly creative think-
ers. They can memorize and regurgitate, but can they think
and act when it really matters? Teaching people what to think
is one thing, but teaching people how to think is altogether
different.

Early in my head coaching career, I walked into the office
of one of my offensive assistant coaches and said, "Tell me what
your philosophy is for a red-zone offense."

The coach eyed me anxiously and said he'd be right back.
He returned with three fat playbooks, two from colleges and
one from the NFL.

"There are a couple of good ideas in here," he said, picking
up one of the books.

"I'm not interested in what's in there. I am interested in
what you think," I said.

He couldn't give me an answer. This smart guy and solid-
enough coach had no opinion.

Periodically, I like to challenge the people on my staff, making an impromptu visit to their office and saying, "Take fifteen

minutes to think, write down one idea that you believe would improve our program."

Some guys give insightful answers. A remarkable number come up with very little at all. Nine years ago in Florida, I put this challenge to Steve Addazio, now the head coach at Boston College, and he came back with the best response I've ever heard. He wrote, "As a unit, we are going to totally buy into the fact that we all trust and are accountable for that guy going into that game and everybody is going to have ownership in that." Those words are on a sign in our football complex to this day. The idea became the basis for the power of the unit—a vital component of what we do and what we are about.

I love to challenge our coaches every day. I love for people to tell me what they think. And if they want to disagree, that's even better. As it says in Proverbs, iron sharpens iron. Out of the sharpening process come better ideas and more committed performance. I don't want yes-men around me. I want people who've thought stuff through and are bringing it to me because they think it will make us better. A big part of being a true leader is being open to new ideas. And those ideas come from thinking.

Dan Mullen, my former assistant at Florida who is now the head coach at Mississippi State, used to challenge me every day, multiple times a day. Dan was so tenacious that there were times I had to leave the office for a short while just to keep him from taking up my entire day. Dan's mind never stopped working. He was always searching for a way to be better and to make his team better. He constantly had suggestions about the spread offense, ways to make it more of a headache for defenses. I knew it wouldn't be long before that quality would earn him a chance to run his own program.

One of my favorite coaching days of the year came to me as a direct result of taking time to think. It was March 2006. Billy Donovan, a friend and neighbor of mine, was the head coach of the University of Florida basketball team and he invited Shelley and me to the Final Four in Indianapolis. It was the first time I'd been at a national championship event. Led by Joakim Noah, Florida had a great run in the tournament, beat George Mason University in the semifinals, and then played UCLA for the championship in the RCA Dome. Late in the final game on that Monday night, Florida had a comfortable lead, and I got a text message from the director of operations for the basketball team. He told me that Billy wanted me to join them in the locker room.

I started shaking. It was that overwhelming and exciting to me—the chance to take this in. I left my seat and went underneath the stands. The Gator fans were already going wild. I was escorted into a side door of the locker room. They were unloading cases of Sprite (no champagne for college players) and then I could hear the countdown. Ten . . . nine . . . eight. By the time the buzzer sounded, I was numb. Then here came the guys and Billy and his staff, piling into the locker room, hugging and laughing and pouncing on each other. This was such a great team, a true team. These players loved each other and loved their coaches. Standing in the corner as I watched all of this joy and closeness play out before me, I welled up with tears. Until then, I had only imagined what it looked like and what it might feel like to win a national championship, but I didn't know. Now, I knew. Now it wasn't theory anymore. The testimony was right in front of me and it was mind blowing. It was so powerful. It was a game changer.

On the flight home to Gainesville, the championship locker room scene was all I could think about. I kept asking myself, "How can I get my team in that locker room? How can I give them the same experience I had?" That's how our Champions Day was born.

Champions Day is when we give our guys a taste of winning it all. I know I talked earlier about how I never make winning a championship a goal and don't even bring up the topic to my players. That is true. We go after Nine Units Strong every day. We pursue relentless effort, competitive excellence, and the power of the unit every single day. Champions Day is different. Champions Day is about creating a vision, a crystal-clear picture of what winning a championship looks like and feels like. The centerpiece of Champions Day is a video presentation that shows champions in a variety of sports celebrating in all of their glory.

There's Joe Namath holding up his ring from Super Bowl III. There's John Madden and Phil Villapiano telling stories about the 1976 championship team. There's Tom Brady and the New England Patriots, Ray Lewis and the Baltimore Ravens, LeBron James and the Miami Heat, and, of course, it features Michael Jordan and the Chicago Bulls. It's a nonstop display of champions. This unique day's purpose is to give every player and every unit leader a chance to observe testimony of the amount of work, commitment, and sheer toughness it takes to win a championship. Then the video takes you inside the winners' locker room because until you've experienced that magical moment, there is nothing like it. To close the day, we have a special guest, someone who has won a championship, speak to our team in order to drive home how special an experience it was for him and his teammates. Billy Donovan came in once. We've also had Teddy Bruschi, Tony Dungy, Bob Knight, and Doc Rivers, all of whom had incredible stories to tell. Doc's Celtics won twenty-four games in 2006–7 and was the second-worst team in the NBA. A year later, they went 66–16, had to survive two seven-game series against the Atlanta Hawks and the Cleveland Cavaliers, then beat the Los Angeles Lakers to win the NBA title. Doc brought along his own video to show how his team responded during those incredibly difficult series. It was as if we were all right there alongside Kevin Garnett, Ray Allen, and Paul Pierce. What a tremendous lesson.

A while back, I was introduced to the work of a man named William Deresiewicz, a gifted author and essayist who gave a lecture at the United States Military Academy at West Point titled "Solitude and Leadership." His central point was that true leadership comes from within. It comes from a deep introspection into your beliefs. But if you can't put aside distractions long enough to be alone in reflection, formulate your own ideas and opinions, then you are handicapping your ability to think, make decisions, and lead. As your problems become more challenging and unique, your thinking needs to become more original. Real-world solutions require real-world leadership. Standard, conventional, cookie-cutter thinking will not enable you to be the leader that your situation requires.

"Thinking means concentrating on one thing long enough to develop an idea about it," Deresiewicz writes. "Not learning other people's ideas, or memorizing a body of information, however much those may sometimes be useful. Developing your own ideas. In short, thinking for yourself. You simply cannot do that in bursts of twenty seconds at a time, constantly interrupted by Facebook messages, or Twitter tweets, or fiddling with your iPod, or watching something on YouTube."

Deresiewicz goes on to talk about how Army officers must routinely confront issues that are far beyond what most people ever contend with. He says that the way to cultivate the strength and wisdom to do the right thing is through deep, fully engaged, solitary thinking.

"The time to start preparing is now," he says. "Waiting until you have to confront them in practice would be like waiting for your first firefight to learn how to shoot your weapon. Once the situation is upon you, it's too big. You have to be prepared in advance. You need to know, already, who you are and what you believe: not what the Army believes, not what your peers believe, but what you believe.

"It seems to me that solitude is the very essence of leadership. The position of the leader is ultimately an intensely solitary, even intensely lonely, one. However many people you may consult, you are the one who has to make the hard decisions. And at such moments, all you really have is yourself."

The solitude that William Deresiewicz writes about has shaped how I approach leading the Ohio State football program. Whether you are working on a game plan or a business plan, there's no doubt that being an effective leader requires independent thought. You need to think in order to have clarity of purpose, to understand what your priorities are, and what you need to do to help your players maximize their potential.

Sometimes great leadership demands space and doing nothing. It took me a long time to learn that. I used to be a terrible delegator. There is great conceit in believing that there's no way the job will get done right if I don't do it. When I was at Florida I was almost obsessed with taking it all on. Sure, we had success, but ultimately it wore me down and impaired my ability to lead the program.

I used to love to play chess when I was a kid. I would play with my father all the time. I loved the challenge of thinking hard, trying to anticipate as many moves ahead as possible. It's mind-boggling to know that an international master such as Bobby Fischer could look at the board for five seconds and know the next five or six moves he would need to make.

The greatest visionaries in every field have that gift for looking ahead. They don't react. They see, they think, and then they respond. In the mid-2000s, Steve Jobs and his team at Apple hated using conventional flip phones and the smartphones that were invading the market.

They decided that they could build a better phone. As they

were designing what would become the iPhone, they had a critical engineering problem to solve. The ubiquitous iPods at the time featured the click wheel to quickly scroll through and navigate the device. Initially, they thought this would be a great way to navigate contacts on a phone as well. However, a new, relatively unused touch screen technology had emerged that enabled tactile, interactive navigation. Jobs looked at the market and saw something nobody else saw. And the world has never been the same since.

An example of how Dan Gilbert's mind works is his "Bullet Time" idea. Every week he gives Quicken's information technology department four hours of break time simply to think of ideas that might help the company. One of the most successful businessmen in the country believes so strongly in the power of thinking that he frees up time to let his people do it. He described how earlier in his career he used to drive his people just to find the broken things and fix them. But as his companies have grown, he has shifted his train of thought to challenging his employees to come up with better ideas. He described himself as being obsessed with finding a better way and said, "Even when things are going good, we constantly challenge our people to look through a different prism, be creative, be innovative and find a different way."

On the other hand, when leaders don't look ahead and think boldly, the consequences can be disastrous. A generation ago, Radio Shack was a pioneer in the electronics retail industry, then let the whole burgeoning marketplace pass them by. For decades, Converse had the serious-basketball-player market to itself, but the company didn't seem to have any vision about where the industry was going or what it needed to do to stay ahead of the field. A young Phil Knight almost had to beg for an audience with the CEO of Converse back in the day, before going on to buy the company and completely rejuvenate the brand.

Here's the bottom line: exceptional leaders think about common things in an uncommon way.

After the difficult defeats to end the 2013 season, I was confronted with a situation where I needed to apply the very R Factor tools that I was teaching to my team. The solution to our problems was only going to be found Above the Line. It was imperative that I think with intention, purpose, and skill. Nothing productive would have happened with Below the Line thinking. In fact, had I reacted Below the Line it would have only made things worse. I had been down that road before and did not want to go there again. So I applied the R Factor disciplines to the situation. I pressed pause, got my mind right, stepped up, adjusted and adapted.

I spent a great deal of time in solitary thinking trying to get to the root causes of our problems. In order to think deeply, though, it is necessary to eliminate the filters that screen out the realities you don't want to see. I asked myself the hard questions: What's *really* going on here? What do we need to do differently? What do I need to do differently? What options are available to me?

I knew we had really good players and a really good staff, but we weren't where we needed to be. We weren't Nine Units Strong.

By taking time to think, I was able to find solutions.

I was able to do what leaders do. Lead.

||||||||||||||||

Chapter Nine: Think Like a Leader Playbook

- Invest the time to think. Make it a priority. Leaders think deeply, originally, and often, bravely.

- When things aren't going right, the most important thing you can do is slow down, go deep, and figure out why.

- Encourage your people to bring new ideas to you. And when they do, listen.

- Exceptional leaders think about common things in an uncommon way.

||||||||||||||||

TEN

The Power of Belief

I've always recognized the power of belief, but the 2014 season confirmed it almost daily. After we lost at home by two touchdowns to Virginia Tech, we dropped to No. 24 in the polls and you could fit the number of people who thought we would do anything that season in the corner of my office.

We had issues, for sure. Our offensive line was in disarray, our quarterback was an unknown entity, our special teams were spotty, and our defense was inconsistent. And yet our guys continued to believe. I think it had everything to do with our training to stay Above the Line. We had trained to answer every difficult event with a strong response. Our culture demanded it.

Belief, I have come to learn, is a critical component in success. Research shows that the highest levels of human performance are empowered by the deepest levels of belief. When a player practices and plays with belief, he performs faster, smarter, and better.

Why? First of all, belief creates vision. It enables you to see possibilities that others do not see. It sees not only the goal it wants to achieve, but the pathway—the effort and action—that is required to accomplish that goal. A player who believes sees himself training, practicing, performing, and achieving. He sees himself competing and winning with such powerful focus that he ignores all distractions and doubters.

Because of this mental clarity, elite performers win in their minds first.

Belief also creates strength of will. Because they believe, elite performers have enormous competitive drive, and that is what makes them relentless. Most players say, "I can't." Some players say, "I hope." Players who believe say, "**I will.**" Their mindset is: *I will do the work. I will do my job. I will make the play. No matter how difficult, no matter how big the challenge, I will do whatever it takes for as long as it takes.* Their belief empowers them with unshakable resolve and determination. It is what animates their ability to respond to any situation with toughness and tenacity. They have a never-quit, never-give-in mindset. They are the top 10 percenters.

Strength of will is not about the commitment to start; it's about the commitment to continue. It's about the many recommitments that are necessary to sustain the journey when it gets difficult, tedious, and painful. In other words, when you face the grind, it's saying "I will" when it gets hard.

Another thing that belief fortifies is your resilience. Resilience is what enables you to bounce back from adversity. It's about making your R stronger than any E you face. When confronted with difficult situations, elite performers waste zero energy worrying or engaging in BCD behavior. Their belief-driven resilience gets them through it and actually makes them stronger. You are only as strong as the challenges you have overcome.

Randy Pausch, the author of *The Last Lecture,* wrote this about adversity:

> *The brick walls are there for a reason. The brick walls are not there to keep us out. The brick walls are there to give us a chance to show how badly we want something. The brick walls are there to stop the people who don't want it badly enough.*

Belief does one more thing that is unique in human performance: it ignites and activates. It unleashes you. Because it is so sharply focused, it blows through doubt and distractions and empowers you to perform at the highest possible level.

Under competitive pressure, your performance will either be enhanced by strong belief or compromised by weak belief. Many athletes work very hard developing physical capabilities yet fail to take full advantage of those capabilities because they haven't paid the same attention to building their minds. It's the R Factor principle we talked about earlier in this book: under pressure, you don't rise to the occasion; you rise or fall to the level of your training.

There's one more bonus to belief: it doesn't just work for

great individual performance. It is an activator of great team performance. On a team, belief is a force multiplier. One man believes and the man next to him believes, and before you know it, it grows exponentially. One of the most powerful forces on earth is a brotherhood of men bonded together by a shared belief in each other and their mission. An elite team has an elite level of belief. It has a vision of where it's going, and the deep strength of will and resilience to get there. For Ohio State football, belief drives our ability to be Nine Units Strong.

Tim Kight gave a tremendous talk on the power of belief after our team dinner the night before the Sugar Bowl, and it was just what we needed to hear. I knew we would need belief and everything else in our arsenal to defeat the number one team in the country, college football's perennial powerhouse.

Nobody had more of an appreciation of how good Alabama was than I did. I'd seen it up close, from the sidelines. After the NCAA hit us with the bowl ban in my first season, ESPN asked me if I'd like to work on the telecast of the national championship game between Alabama and Notre Dame. I was on the field at Miami's Sun Life Stadium before the game, paying close attention to the Alabama players' warm-up, and I was blown away by everything I saw. The pace. The crispness of the execution. The unmistakable we're-here-on-a-mission demeanor.

Alabama was better than we were at that point. The evidence was right in my face. It had won three of the last four national championships, a feat that the school hadn't even accomplished under Bear Bryant. Up and down the roster they had size and speed with playmakers all over the field. My goal every year is to have the best coaching staff in America, leading the best players in America. But seeing what I was seeing on the sidelines of Sun Life Stadium, there was no way I could say that, and I wanted to make sure everybody in our program knew it. So I grabbed my phone and sent a text to every player and every unit leader, right there from the sidelines:

The Chase is on immediately, because we are not the best team in the country. Alabama is.

And just in case anybody thought I was overhyping them, Alabama then went on to beat Notre Dame 42–14. Before the confetti was done flying that night, The Chase was on. The Chase wasn't to beat Alabama; it was to be the best, which in all likelihood meant going through Alabama. The Chase is what drove us, and if you want to use the word *obsession,* I wouldn't argue with you. Soon we had a huge sign over the end of our practice field: THE CHASE. We had another one in Coach Mick's weight room. It was The Chase to close that gap. The Chase to beat the best, so we could become the best. It was purposeful and intentional, and if we did everything we hoped to do—if we were fully aligned and giving our all for each other, and if we were driven and committed to pursuing our shared purpose with Above the Line behavior—I knew in my heart it was within our reach.

We had a month to prepare for Alabama after beating Wisconsin in the Big Ten championship game. Our whole plan was to systematically build belief and motivation. I learned an important lesson from Lou Holtz: when playing a quality opponent, always build them up. We kept telling our players about what I had witnessed at the national championship game a couple of years ago and of how great a team Alabama is. We wanted to make sure our players knew exactly what we would be facing and what a challenge it would be to play them. We wanted them to be ticked off even at the mention of Alabama. We wanted them to play with an edge, driven by a desire to shut up all the people—and there were millions of them—who thought Ohio State was the second best team in the Sugar Bowl.

After that, we gradually changed the narrative, building our guys up, empowering them. We did it initially with a message called "Six Percent," which we introduced with the game still a few weeks out. I got the guys together one day and said: "You don't have to beat Alabama today. You don't have to beat them tomorrow, or even the next day. So you don't have to do everything right now to beat them today. Today, all you need to do is get six percent better. That's all. Give us relentless effort and get six percent better. If every one of you does that every day, by the time the foot hits the ball in the Sugar Bowl, you'll be ready."

Day after day, guys would show up for practice, and we'd keep harping on the Six Percent. You could feel something special building. You could feel belief building. Our players were Above the Line in every aspect of their preparation. You heard no BCD. You saw the bonds of brotherhood growing stronger.

Our players had a growing belief that we were good enough to put The Chase to rest.

But my favorite belief and brotherhood builder before the Sugar Bowl, without a doubt, was the clicker. It was the brainchild of our special teams coach Kerry Coombs and David Trichel, our video coordinator and a master of cinematic motivation. David is from Louisiana, and a couple of years prior to the Sugar Bowl he met up with his father in New Orleans and toured the National World War II Museum. The museum is a short distance from the south Louisiana factories that built Higgins boats—the amphibious vessels that General Eisenhower later said were responsible for winning the war—in the 1940s. The factories produced more than 20,000 Higgins boats by 1943, and they were the key element that enabled one of the largest amphibious operations in military history—the D-Day invasion of Normandy on June 6, 1944. In the early, predawn hours before the landings at Normandy, an estimated thirty thousand paratroopers from the 82nd Airborne dropped in behind enemy lines to disrupt Nazi supply channels and seize strategic positions. Coping with darkness and heavily overcast conditions, many of the paratroopers missed their designated landing zones and were scattered across the French countryside. In order to communicate their locations to one another without blowing their cover, every paratrooper had been given a small brass clicker before jumping. It's a thumb-sized device that gives off a distinct cricketlike sound and was used to covertly determine friend from foe. A paratrooper would click once, and if two clicks were returned, the unidentified soldier was deemed an ally. But if two clicks were not returned, the unidentified soldier was classified as the enemy and contact was made.

It was the perfect theme for the mission we were on.

Special teams are unique because they're comprised of players from different units. For example, we have wide receivers on our punt team and linebackers on our kickoff team. Throughout the entire season, Kerry did a fantastic job at making the players from their respective units feel as if they truly were brothers on special teams.

"We wanted to reinforce the idea that they were a specially chosen unit, a band of brothers, going into battle behind enemy lines," Trichel said. "Those players were so close to each other. They knew the only way they get through that battle, to win that game, was if they fought for each other."

Every special teams player was required to carry his clicker with him at all times. I had one in my pocket, too. Throughout the week leading up to the game, if you passed your brother and he clicked at you, you clicked back twice. If you clicked him first, he'd click back twice. Up and down the hallways of our hotel, at our meals and walk-throughs, guys were clicking away.

At the hotel before our pregame meal, we got another lift. In the Outback Bowl, Wisconsin (the same Wisconsin team we shut out 59–0) beat Auburn (the same Auburn team that had given Alabama a major scare five weeks earlier by putting up 630 yards of offense) in overtime. You can argue that the common-opponent factor is a meaningless measuring stick, but in our players' minds, it helped justify our being there. It sent a powerful message of confirmation that we truly were one of the elite teams in college football.

It was a defining moment in our mental preparation.

I had plenty of reasons to be optimistic and at the top of the list was Cardale Jones. As I watched him in practice in the days leading up to the game, it was as if I were watching a championship-caliber quarterback. The transformation that started in the Wisconsin game was continuing. He was in charge of everything. He was a presence. He was fully engaged and attuned to everything we said. His reads were flawless, his execution too. In the span of a few weeks, a kid who had been a BCD-ing backup had become the starting quarterback of our championship run.

After warm-ups as we gathered in the locker room before the game, I could still sense a palpable tension and nervousness. I wondered whether The Chase theme had been force-fed to them for so long that maybe they were hesitant about what to expect.

Seeing how quiet and tight the mood was, I knew we needed to go right at it. What wins games is not coming up with the right rah-rah speech before a game; it's the months and months of getting your players' minds right and their bodies right. In this case, however, it was clear to me we needed a few positive messages to lower the tension levels.

J. T. Barrett, our injured quarterback, gave a brilliant talk about how sick and tired he was of hearing how great Alabama was, and what an insult it was that Ohio State was 9-

point underdogs. "Everybody do their part, we're gonna win. I promise you that," Barrett said. "If you are not winning, stay here!" He paused for an instant and said it again: "If you are not ready to win, stay here."

Michael Bennett, the defensive lineman, laid it out there for the defense. "Look to the guy to your left, the guy to your right, and the guy behind you. We've watched these guys on film, they ain't better than us, they ain't meaner, they ain't tougher. I've got the meanest, toughest defense on the field right next to me! All game you hit 'em! All game!"

It was minutes before kickoff. I didn't want to pound on the same themes. The guys were stoked now. The quiet was gone. My gut told me it was time to go straight to our culture. Here's what I said:

"Eyes on me real fast. . . . Listen up . . . four to six seconds, A to B. You put your foot in the ground and you go as hard as you can go. That's the secret, that's the whole secret. They know. The whole world knows—four to six, A to B. No secret message today. Take care of each other. You've been trained all your career since you stepped foot on the Ohio State campus for this moment. Let's go get it all. Let's go get it all. You can and you will. For the guy next to you."

My speech lasted twenty-nine seconds. I held my arm up and the guys huddled in, the closest players to me clamping their hands on my raised arm, everybody holding up their arms and shouting, "Nine Strong!"

The last thing I said is the last thing I've said before every game since I was at Bowling Green:

"One, two, three . . . Showtime!" The whole team shouts "Showtime!" with me.

We took the field. The Superdome was electric with noise and anticipation. Just before kickoff, I called the kickoff team up on the sideline and pulled them in close to me. I pulled out my clicker and started clicking.

They went nuts.

On defense, our primary focus was to contain Amari Cooper, who won the Biletnikoff Award as the nation's top receiver. He'd been wrecking opponents all year, especially with short passes that he would turn into long gainers. The game plan was to press him right off the line, take away the easy throws, and force quarterback Blake Sims to make the tougher throws down the field. We thought that if we could limit the big plays and force them to earn their yards every series, we would have a shot. Luke Fickell and Chris Ash, our co–defensive coordinators, did an excellent job game-planning third down situations, giving Alabama different looks that we had not shown previously to confuse the quarterback.

The quarterback is the most unique position in all of sport. They have to know everyone's assignment, make sure the offensive line is in the right protection, give the cadence, receive the snap, make the right read, and deliver the ball. All of this in under two seconds. When confused, there is great potential for a turnover.

The Sugar Bowl didn't exactly unfold the way I had planned. We were moving the ball effectively and yet were down 15 points (21–6) midway through the second quarter because of turnovers and missed opportunities in the red zone. The fact is we were having our way moving the ball against a great team and our guys on defense were playing hard.

Going into the locker room at halftime I was disappointed and thinking about tearing into some guys to shake things up.

Until I saw the first half stats.

I called the team up and said, "Here are the facts—370 yards of offense good guys, 120 yards of offense bad guys. You take care of the ball, this one is over: 370 to 120. Look at me. Nine Units Strong. Get it done!"

Belief? I had plenty of it. I had more of it now than I had before the game. I knew that if we stopped giving the ball away, we'd be fine. We were winning the battle at the line of scrimmage, and we had been the better team through thirty minutes. That was the message at halftime with the score 21–20.

You could feel us coming. I think everybody in the building could feel us coming. We got the ball on our 25 to start the second half. Cardale hit Michael Thomas for 11 yards on first down, then hit Michael again for 8 more yards. Ezekiel Elliott ran for 7 to get us into Alabama territory at the 49, and after an incompletion, Jalin Marshall picked up 2 on a swing pass. So now we had a third-and-eight. In the shotgun, Cardale dropped back as Alabama blitzed. He looked left quickly, then right, where Devin Smith was running a deep sideline route. Cardale let it fly, and as he did the Alabama defensive back slipped and fell. All alone, Devin caught the ball inside the five and took it in for the score. After the extra point, the score was 27–21— our first lead since the score was 3–0.

We weren't close to being done.

Late in the third quarter, Blake Sims had a third-and-seven situation from his own 36. In an obvious passing situation, we came with a zone blitz as defensive end Steve Miller dropped back into coverage. Cooper ran a little curl pattern on the left side. Miller read the play perfectly, saw where Sims was going. He stepped inside Cooper just as the ball arrived at the 41-yard line and ran it all the way in for a touchdown with just over three minutes left in the quarter. Now we were up, 34–21. It was the biggest deficit Alabama had faced all year. With eighteen minutes to play, we had the momentum, and I wanted to be sure we didn't have any kind of lapse and give it right back. We needed a big-time play from our special teams. Right before the kickoff, I called the kickoff team over again. I waited until they were all around me. I locked eyes with as many of the guys as I could. I pulled out the clicker again and started clicking it right in front of their faces.

I have never witnessed a more focused moment.

With the look in their eyes, I knew something big was about to happen. The kickoff team ran past the Alabama blockers, and Bri'onte Dunn and Corey Smith nailed the returner on the 16-yard line. It was brilliant stuff. Courageous stuff. It was purely devotion to their brothers and to the mission that drove Smith and Dunn down the field to make that pivotal play. So often, the difference between winning and losing comes down to a play like that with a margin for error so thin. It was two elite warriors making an elite play.

Alabama did not go away. The Tide made it a one-score

game (34–28), and due to our poor field position and an inability to move the ball, momentum had shifted the Tide's way with under ten minutes left to play.

On first down, the Tide sent Amari Cooper in motion, split out wide left. Sims took the snap and rolled to his right and looked for the tight end in the right corner of the end zone. We blitzed our inside linebackers and had safety Vonn Bell drop to the middle. Bell recognized the play immediately because he'd been studying it for weeks. As the tight end broke for the end zone, Bell undercut his corner route.

"Me and Coach Ash have seen that play over a million times," Bell said. "We knew when they were going to run it."

It was Vonn Bell's version of the backdoor slider. He made a great break on the throw and picked it off right at the goal line. Had Alabama scored, the whole dynamic of the game would have shifted. Vonn made a huge play in a huge moment. So did many of our players, never more so than on third downs. We converted ten of our eighteen third-down opportunities (Cardale had 153 of his 243 passing yards on those plays); Alabama converted on just two of thirteen, thanks in large part to the different looks that Luke and Chris kept giving them. While Cooper did score two touchdowns, he averaged fewer than 8 yards per catch on his nine receptions. You put it all together, and our defensive game plan worked exactly as we'd hoped.

Two possessions later, on our 15-yard line, we ran a stretch play to the left. Zeke put his foot in the ground and made a great upcut off a devastating block by our captain, Evan Spencer, and never stopped running. He went 85 yards for the score and restored our two-touchdown lead. Zeke rushed for a Sugar Bowl record: 230 yards on twenty carries. Alabama had not allowed a runner to go for 100 yards all season. We believed we could run against them, and we were right.

Even then Alabama wasn't done, closing to within 7 points at 42–35. With under two minutes to play, the whole world knew an onside kick was coming. Alabama kicker Adam Griffith chipped a perfect squib 10 yards down the field. We had our best "hands" guys up there, among them Evan Spencer, our senior receiver. Evan was one of those players who made my belief in this team so deep. The son of former OSU standout and NFL running back Tim Spencer, he would do whatever it took to help his unit and his team. Evan was an outstanding blocker and would finish his senior season with just fifteen catches in our fifteen games. Though he may not have put up gaudy numbers, everyone on our team would tell you he was one of the best football players we had, an MVP-type guy to the core. You can't measure everything by numbers. It's easy to forget that in the data-driven world we live in. All Evan did was make plays.

In the first half of the Sugar Bowl, we ran a trick play, and Evan threw a touchdown pass to Michael Thomas. Ezekiel Elliott wouldn't have gone for that 85-yard TD without Evan, who laid a crushing block on the Alabama linebacker closest to the play. And now here came Griffith's fluttering kick. Evan leaped up, arms outstretched, knowing he would get hit. He pulled the ball down in heavy traffic and kept it secure, one of the best examples of guts and poise I'd seen all season. It was a key play that helped save the game.

Alabama got the ball back one more time, on their own 18. There was 1:33 to play.

The Sugar Bowl was going to come down to one last drive.

Sims had pulled off a string of heroic late comebacks. Could he do it again? He completed one pass, then another and another, before scrambling for 12 yards and a first down at midfield. Then he hit the tight end on a quick out for 8 yards. The ball was on our 42. There were fifteen seconds left. Alabama had at least two, maybe three, more plays. The secondary had played a strong game for the most part. We needed someone to make a play, or we might have an entire offseason to figure out why we couldn't hold a two-score lead in the fourth quarter.

Sims took a deep shot down the left sideline. We figured they would target Cooper, the top receiver in the country, in such an urgent situation, but Sims's throw went to DeAndrew White in the left corner. Cornerback Eli Apple was with White step for step with Bell helping out, peeling away from Cooper when the ball went in the air. Eli made a fantastic pass breakup, nearly intercepting the ball, and now eight seconds remained. We thought they might have time for two more plays, so we didn't commit to a full victory coverage in the end zone to defend against a Hail Mary. Our greatest concern was Cooper, because he'd been the game breaker the whole season. And again, Sims did not go his way, launching a ball into a crowd in the right side of the end zone, where there were five Ohio State defenders surrounding two Alabama receivers. Tyvis Powell emerged from the crowd and picked it off. He was exactly where he was supposed to be, the same way Steve Miller was when he put Sims under heavy pressure on his desperation heave, and the same way that Evan was on the onside kick. It came down to great players making great plays. It came down to believing in each other and our ability to respond.

I looked up at the clock. It showed nothing but zeroes. We had beaten mighty Alabama.

Seeing was believing.

||||||||||||||||||

Chapter Ten: The Power of Belief Playbook

- The highest levels of performance are empowered by the deepest levels of belief.

- Belief creates vision. It sees the invisible. It sees the goal and the pathway that are required to accomplish the goal.

- Belief creates strength of will. It animates the ability to respond to any situation with extraordinary toughness, tenacity, and perseverance.

- Belief creates resilience, the ability to respond and bounce back from adversity.

- Belief ignites and activates. It gives you full access to your talents and abilities.

- Under competitive pressure, strong belief will pull your performance up; weak belief will pull it down.

- Belief is not simply about individual performance. It is an essential element of exceptional team performance. Shared belief empowers a team to operate at full capacity. Nine Units Strong.

||||||||||||||||||

ELEVEN

The Chase Is Complete

Our collective belief couldn't have been any higher after the Alabama game. Look at our recent body of work. Not only had we won twelve straight games, we'd beaten Wisconsin by 59 points for the Big Ten championship, and then beaten the top-ranked team in the country in the Sugar Bowl as a big underdog. By now, the Virginia Tech game didn't even feel as if it were part of the same season. It wasn't just that we were winning, it was the way we were winning, with huge contributions from every unit—Nine Strong. After struggling early, the offensive line had become a close unit and was blocking incredibly well, dominating against two of the best defenses in the country, Wisconsin and Alabama. Ezekiel Elliott had run for 450 yards and four touchdowns in the last two games alone, averaging more than 11 yards per carry. When you consider that it's outstanding for a running back to average

5 yards per carry, it gives you an idea of how exceptional Zeke had been.

Our premier defensive players, Darron Lee, Joey Bosa, and Vonn Bell, were at the top of their games, and the receiving corps—especially Evan Spencer, Devin Smith, Michael Thomas, and Jalin Marshall—had emerged as a major force that made it impossible for defenses to load the box to try to stop Zeke.

And our third-string quarterback, Cardale Jones, wasn't doing too badly, either, growing by the day, continuing his transformation from BCD-prone backup to a championship-caliber quarterback.

In more than a quarter-century of coaching, I've never seen a team that has overcome more or made more progress from the beginning of the season to the end. From a bad early-season loss to crippling injuries to a devastating tragedy, we had dealt with all manner of hardship, and kept moving forward. We did not complain or give in to despair. We didn't pay attention to the multitudes who said we were done. We came to work each day, and we got better. We worked hard to get and stay Above the Line. No matter what events we were hit with, our responses were strong, our alignment was set, and the bond among us grew only stronger as the year went forward.

It was deeply gratifying to witness this team's growth and maturation, but this was no time for complacency. Our job was not finished; The Chase was not complete. We had to keep pushing to be better every day, every one of us. You stay in the same place, you fall behind.

With Oregon, we were going against an opponent we had great respect for. It had the Heisman Trophy winner, Marcus Mariota, at quarterback, and had just manhandled undefeated Florida State and looked unbeatable in doing it. Sure, we had just slain the giant, but now our sights shifted to a whole different challenge—and the only game left on our schedule.

At the hotel in Dallas, our players went about their business as professionals. Almost every day I would tell our players to imagine that they were elite soldiers on a mission. "Get that visual right now," I'd say. "You're in the helicopters. You have been given a mission, a directive, an assignment. You've got your guys there beside you. You're going in."

When you are up against Oregon, the biggest challenge is getting accustomed to the pace of play, which is arguably the fastest in college football. We had a theme for the whole week of practice: *Eliminate 16*. Sixteen seconds is the amount of time the Oregon offense takes between plays. Sixteen seconds, and then they are coming at you again, and the longer the game goes on, the greater the toll it takes. In the Pac-12 championship game, Oregon scored 28 points in the second half against Arizona. Against Florida State in the Rose Bowl, Oregon had 41 points after halftime. We knew for us to win, we needed to be ready for their pace. We needed to practice at their pace. We had play clocks set to sixteen seconds on both ends of our practice field. We had the number posted all over the Woody Hayes Athletic Center. We even had two shot clocks frozen on the number 16 at both ends of our hotel dining room. Guys could not get away from No. 16, to the point that Coach Mick tore the No. 16 jersey off reserve defensive back Cam Burrows, giving him No. 8 instead. He wore the number in the game.

We were determined to eliminate 16.

In practice, we had two scout teams taking snaps, one after another.

"You put the clock up there and try to get it running as fast as possible," linebacker Joshua Perry said. "It's trained us to make the play and get up and save the celebration for when we get off the field. You turn to the sideline, get the call, and then immediately refocus on what's happening on the field."

We knew containing Mariota was key. He's a great runner who can shred your whole defense when he's able to get in the open field. You can defend a play superbly and he'll make a move, then cut back and go for 18 yards. Against Florida State, he ran eight times for 62 yards, many of them at pivotal points in the game. We wanted to make sure we set the edge to contain outside runs, aiming to cut down on his ability to improvise. We were confident that we had the size and strength up front to control the line of scrimmage. We thought that if we kept Mariota from running wild and played sound defense, we could force them into third-and-long situations, which is not what their offense is built for. The more we could force them into those situations, the more it would slow down the pace of the game, and that would work in our favor.

Every game day we have a pregame motivational video that the team and staff watch together at the hotel right before we head to the stadium. I give a brief message, followed by the video. This video features season highlights set to music and concludes with a specific movie clip. I had met with David Trichel before we left for Dallas and told him exactly what I wanted.

My message to the team was about how for the past year, our clarity of purpose was not to make it to the national championship, but about getting to Nine Units Strong. If we finish this game Nine Units Strong, we'll be the champions of college football. As I closed my message to the team, I said, "You're about to see a clip at the end of the video about the unit who took out Osama bin Laden. They are the best of the best in the military. They are the elite. They were given a mission, and they accomplished that mission. At the end of the clip, after they killed him, one of the guys looks at the shooter and asked, 'Do you even realize what you just did?' and you can see in the shooter's face that at that moment, he understood the gravity of what just happened. Tonight, when the clock strikes zero, you're going to look around at your guys, at your unit, and you're going to ask, 'Do you even realize what you just did?'" I paused for a moment.

"You'll be able to look right back at him and say, 'We're national champions.'"

Almost in unison I could hear an exhale of released tension from the team. They were ready. They understood the gravity of what was at stake. They knew that every hardship they had been through and overcome during the past year had brought them here. They knew what needed to be done.

From the hotel to AT&T Stadium, our players maintained

their focus. As we walked from the buses to the locker room to the field, I felt the same presence and confidence coming from the team as I had in New Orleans. They had been trained well. I looked at the players gathered around their unit leaders and knew that the brotherhood they had been building was now stronger than ever. Our culture was about to be put into the crucible one final time.

It didn't take long to find out that you can prepare all you want for the pace, but seeing it in front of you is a different deal. Oregon took the opening kickoff and went 75 yards in eleven plays, in two minutes, thirty-nine seconds. They just carved us up. Mariota ran for a pivotal first down and turned a broken play into a touchdown, scrambling and firing to Keanon Lowe to finish it off.

Minutes into the championship game, sixteen had not only not been eliminated; sixteen had run right through us. Oregon looked no different from the juggernaut that had steamrolled Florida State. It was the worst possible way to start the game, but here was the most amazing thing: up and down the Ohio State sideline—full of players, coaches, and staffers—nobody was panicking after that drive.

There was only one person who was concerned.

Me.

On my headset, I told offensive coordinator Tom Herman, "We may need to score one hundred tonight." I couldn't believe after all our work that they made it look so easy. Was this how it was going to go?

I went over to talk to Luke Fickell and Chris Ash, and they

were completely unfazed. I looked at the players on the defensive unit and they looked the same way. The message from all of them was: *"We've got it. Don't worry. We're well prepared. We're going to be fine."*

"Oregon is a fast-strike team," Chris Ash said. "That's how their offense works. We knew the pace was going to take a little time to get used to. We also knew it was a long game. There was no sense of panic and nobody was saying we should scrap our plan and do something different. I really believed we'd be fine once we settled in."

The collective calm around me brought me in off the ledge. I was able to press pause and take in the belief of our players and coaches. I didn't rip anybody, didn't throw anything. When I was younger, I would've gone ballistic, but when it came down to it I had so much trust in all these guys that I came to see I was overreacting.

The entire tenor of the game shifted almost immediately. We forced Oregon to punt on their next possession, and though we got pinned at our own 3-yard line, Cardale—now a veteran of three career starts—hit a pair of 26-yard passes to Jalin Marshall and Corey Smith. Marshall powered his way to a first down on a big fourth-and-two, and then Zeke blew through a big hole in the line, made a couple of beautiful moves, and was off on a 33-yard touchdown run to conclude a 97-yard march.

The score was 7–7. We had our footing now. On the sideline, I was thinking, *We've settled in. We're ready for battle. Let's go.*

As we prepared for Oregon, we viewed the game as a battle of our culture versus their culture. We had high regard for

Oregon's explosiveness and all their weapons—how could you not?—but we nonetheless believed that our culture would prevail. We believed that nobody had trained harder than we had, or had been through more. We believed that no matter what happened in the game, we would summon whatever R we would need to get through it. As they say in the military, when contact is made, you revert to your training. And we had great faith in the rigor of our training. In so many ways, this game was a microcosm of what I've long believed and what we looked at earlier: relentless effort will win out over mistakes every time. We had four turnovers in the national championship game, and we had them at terrible times. We kept fighting. We never let up for a second, regardless of the circumstances, and a sequence early in the second quarter proved it.

Cardale fumbled on a running play and Oregon recovered on its own 39. Mariota took them down the field in typical breakneck fashion, completing five passes and moving 51 yards, all the way down to our 10-yard line. We were up by a touchdown. It would be a huge momentum swing if Oregon finished off the drive with a TD. After two runs and an incomplete pass, the Ducks had fourth-and-goal on the 3. They were the most explosive offense in college football, so we weren't surprised that they decided to go for it.

Mariota took the snap and handed off to running back Thomas Tyner. A hole briefly opened, but then Curtis Grant came flying in and put a hit on him, and Adolphus Washington fought off a block and got help from Tyvis Powell, and the two of them brought Tyner down on the 1-yard line.

It was goal-line defense at its finest.

Oregon had had a prime opportunity to tie the score, but our defense rose up when it mattered most. Without that stop, who knows what direction the game goes?

We took a 21–10 lead into the half, before Oregon scored 10 points in the third quarter, suddenly making it a 1-point game midway through the third quarter. It was another critical point in the game, arguably our most important drive of the year. It was the moment that we are always talking about; elite competitors come through when it matters most.

We took over on our 25. Zeke pounded for 12 yards on two runs. Cardale connected with Michael Thomas for 17 yards on the right sideline, Michael doing a great tightrope dance to extend the play, the first of four completions on the drive. Zeke had a punishing run for a first down on third-and-one. A few plays later Cardale had an even more punishing run, blasting through 550 pounds of Oregon defenders on third-and-three. It was his will versus their will, and Cardale wasn't going to be stopped. You could feel it even on the sideline. Moments later, Zeke scored on a great 9-yard run, a spectacular finish to a 12-play, 75-yard march that consumed almost seven minutes. It was a sledgehammer drive; we came right at them with our power and dared them to stop us, and they couldn't.

Back up by eight (28–20) as the fourth quarter began, we needed a defensive statement. You don't get in shootouts with a team like Oregon and win. After Mariota completed a 20-yard pass to Lowe, linebacker Darron Lee tossed aside a blocker and stuffed running back Royce Freeman. One play later, Mariota thought he had receiver Dwayne Stanford open over the middle, except that Darron dropped back and made a diving deflection—a dazzling athletic play. Now it was third-and-ten, just where we wanted them. We forced another incompletion and a punt, and then we went on another long drive.

The Oregon Ducks never crossed midfield during the entire fourth quarter.

All game our offensive line opened holes and did a great job protecting Cardale. Our gap blocking was brilliant. Thirteen times in the game we ran a counter play, selling a sweep to Jalin Marshall with right guard Pat Elflein pulling along with tight end Jeff Heuerman to open up huge holes. After his 220 yards against Wisconsin and 230 against Alabama, Zeke outdid himself, going for 246 yards and four touchdowns against Oregon. It was one of the best three-game performances by a running back in the history of college football. With under a minute to play, Zeke scored the final touchdown of the game. Just before I took off my headset, Tom Herman asked me one last question, "Coach, do you even realize what you just did?"

Time wound down, and a timeless football truth took hold. If you want to shut down an offensive powerhouse, what works 100 percent of the time is not letting that offense have the ball. Our total time of possession was thirty-seven minutes, twenty-nine seconds; Oregon's was twenty-two minutes, thirty-one seconds.

That was how we Eliminated 16.

Zeke ran the ball twenty-five times in the second half alone, and we ran it sixty-one times overall—about 50 percent more than we did against Alabama. Cardale threw the ball with tremendous touch and accuracy in the game, but with the way we were overpowering them on the ground, there was no reason not to continue the pounding and keep the clock moving.

And move it we did—down to three minutes, and two, and one, and soon the scoreboard in AT&T Stadium in Arlington, Texas, showed nothing but the final score: Ohio State 42, Oregon 20.

I got the obligatory Gatorade bath and hugs and handshakes, but the euphoria I felt wasn't just because we had Eliminated 16, or validated the belief we had in ourselves, or even that we'd won the first championship in the College Football Playoff era. All of those things were great, but for me what made this season most special was the journey our players had made to get to the mountaintop. The work and the training, the laughter and the tears, the triumphs and the adversity—all of it flashed through my mind even as the confetti fell and I made my way to the stage. We had fought so hard to get and stay Above the Line. My national championship teams at Florida were phenomenal and will forever be special to me. Now, this Ohio State team had earned a special place all its own. From a leadership perspective, it gets no better than that. A leader is someone who inspires and empowers people to get to places that they wouldn't be able to reach otherwise, sure, but you also need to have people who are willing to be led. You have to have people who have high character and the courage and strength and resilience to push through pain and fight off frustration, who want to be elite at what they do, and who understand that Above the Line behavior is what is going to get them there.

You need to have great players who play great—people who don't just talk about being team first, but who live it every day, who go into battle for the man on their left and the man on their right and can't imagine doing anything that would ever let them down. The 2014 Ohio State Buckeyes embodied all of these things.

We were champions. We were Nine Units Strong.

It was an honor to be their coach.

EPILOGUE

‖‖‖‖‖‖‖‖‖‖‖‖‖‖‖‖‖‖‖‖‖‖‖‖‖‖‖‖‖

In football and in life, you want to get better every day. There is no room for complacency or looking back on past accomplishments. In my thirteen years as a head coach, I've had the great fortune to coach great players, work with great assistant coaches, and win three national championships. Do you know how much time I am going to spend thinking about this during the 2015 season?

Zero.

Every twenty-four hours is a fresh opportunity to get better. That is what inspires me and drives me, not only as a coach but also as a husband, a father, and a human being.

It does not mean life always unfolds that way. There are setbacks. There are frustrations. There are doubts and defeats, and there isn't a human being alive who has immunity. I will have them. You will have them. What it all comes down to is how you respond when those setbacks and frustrations hit you. Will you give up and figure that it's just not your time? Will you lament that things never seem to work out the way you want them to? Or will you dig in and do the work necessary to get and stay Above the Line?

Here's the great secret about leadership: it's not about you. It's about making other people better. Leadership is more about trust you have earned than the authority you have been granted. You must earn the right for people to follow you. It is about equipping people with the tools necessary to get and stay Above the Line. It is about maximizing their talent and their lives. It's one of the greatest gifts you could ever have because you are doing something that has far more importance than the outcome of a football game. You are stretching people, helping them change and grow. You are taking people to places they never thought they would reach. You are helping them live better lives. Think about that. It's deeply humbling to be able to have that kind of impact.

We've spent scores of pages talking about leadership and culture; my hope is that it has given you some helpful ideas and insights that can be applied to your own circumstances. If you take nothing else away from this book, I hope it has given you an appreciation that leadership skills are not just handed to you because you might have a big title and a lot of people under you. There is a lot of pseudo-leadership in this country—would-be movers and shakers who believe leadership automatically comes bundled with authority. It is simply not so. Just as athletes need to take reps to get proficient at their skills, leaders need to take reps, too. It must be an intentional and dedicated pursuit, a single-minded mission to reach inside people, unlock their potential, and inspire them to reach a new level. Your commitment to it, your level of engagement and energy will determine the results you get. Be open to new ideas. Live, listen, and learn. You can't learn what you think you already know; the day you think you know it all is the day you start falling behind. Remember, you can't lead people to a place that you are not going to as well. If it isn't happening *in* you, it won't happen *through* you.

I had one of the most remarkable and exhilarating years of my life in 2014. What made it special was not just the way it ended, raising the championship trophy as confetti fell all over AT&T Stadium in Arlington, Texas, but the journey we took and the challenges we overcame along the way. There can't be change without challenge, or growth without discomfort. After we lost three of four games and lost one star quarterback and then another, among other key players, most of the college football world wrote us off. But it was when we were confronted with our most challenging events that we did our best work and produced our greatest responses. That was when our players and staff truly showed how our culture could overcome adversity. They refused to quit. They pushed through pain and discouragement and hardship. They embraced the brotherhood of trust and kept at it for one another, and they achieved an unforgettable outcome.

I've learned a tremendous amount about leadership in the last year. I also know there is so much more to learn. Whatever might lie ahead for me as a coach and a leader, one thing I know is that my relentless quest for improvement never ends. I want to be elite and lead the people who are in my charge to be elite also.

You have a purpose in life. If you are clear about what that purpose is, then these tools can help you fulfill it and enable you to better serve those around you. If you're not sure about your life's purpose, then use the knowledge and experience you've just read to help guide you on your path discovering it. My hope is that what I've written in this book will help you on your journey.

Our Purpose Is Clear:

NINE UNITS STRONG

I am a member of an elite team of warriors, a group of men with an uncommon commitment to a common purpose.

Our brotherhood has been forged through rigorous training, unrelenting discipline, and painful adversity. We train to fight and we fight to win.

I have an obligation to hold my unit accountable and be held accountable for our actions.

I will do my job. I will hold my point.

Nothing is more important than my connection to my unit.

My actions, my words, and my attitude are all in alignment with our purpose.

I trust my unit leader and his vision for our unit.

I seek no glory for myself but for my unit and for my teammates.

To be a brother in such a unit is a privilege that I must earn every single day.

The culture of our unit begins with my character.

The team's core values are my core values.

I am not perfect and strive to fix the problem areas in my life.

I behave in a way that shows my unit that they can count on me in the most difficult of situations.

My response will be greater than any event I face.

I am that man.

ACKNOWLEDGMENTS

It has been an honor and a privilege to coach some of the greatest young men I have ever been around. I am deeply appreciative to the players who have made my twenty-nine years of coaching so rewarding.

The process of writing this book has taught me that being an author has a lot in common with coaching a football team. You need key contributions from many people for the result to come together, beginning with my agent and friend, Trace Armstrong of CAA, along with his CAA colleague Simon Green, who found an excellent publisher in Penguin Press and an outstanding editor in Scott Moyers.

A special thank-you to Wayne Coffey for breathing life into this story. He spent many hours away from home, and I appreciate the sacrifices he made to make this book happen.

Much of what I believe, as a coach and a man, was learned from four great mentors: Earle Bruce, Lou Holtz, Sonny Lubick, and Bob Davie. I am grateful for having had the opportunity to learn from them. Thank you to Bill Belichick for being the friend and coach that you are. Likewise, Phil Knight has been a great friend and someone I can count on for insight when I've had to make big decisions. He truly represents Nike's mission statement—to bring inspiration and innovation to every athlete in the world.

Roger Goodell, I appreciate your friendship and our real-life conversations. I've known Dan Gilbert and Jamie Dimon only a relatively short time—but long enough to know they are great men and leaders, a well of influence and knowledge who have had a huge impact on me.

I've had the good fortune to work for four preeminent athletic directors, from Gene Smith at Ohio State to Jeremy Foley at Florida, along with Chris Hill and Paul Krebs at Utah and Bowling Green, respectively—all exceptional leaders in their own right. I have been fortunate to have had some of the most talented coaching staffs in college football over the years. I am extremely proud to have worked with Kyle Whittingham, Steve Addazio, Dan Mullen, Doc Holliday, Gary Andersen, Charlie Strong, Tim Beckman, Tom Herman, Everett Withers, Gregg Brandon, and Dan McCarney, all of whom are currently running their own programs. I have also been blessed with talented and loyal assistants such as Chuck Heater, Greg Mattison, Greg Studrawa, John Hevesy, among others, who were no less instrumental in our success.

My 2014 coaching staff was as good as it gets. Without them there's no way we would've been Nine Units Strong or National Champions. With the utmost respect, I am forever grateful to

ACKNOWLEDGMENTS

Luke Fickell, Chris Ash, Larry Johnson, Kerry Coombs, Tom Herman, Ed Warinner, Stan Drayton, Zach Smith, and Tim Hinton. Six of my most trusted and long-standing assistants are Mickey Marotti, Brian Voltolini, Hiram Defries, Mark Pantoni, Ryan Stamper, and Amy Nicol; they have been more loyal than I could have ever expected, and I wouldn't be where I am without them. My 2014 support staff worked long and hard behind the scenes to keep things moving smoothly and should know that they are never taken for granted. They included Kenny Parker, Jeff Uhlenhake, Anthony Schlegel, Phil Matusz, Vince Okruch, Greg Gillum, Stan Jefferson, Doug Calland, and Fernando Lovo.

My leadership cabinet—Mickey Marotti, Tim Kight, and David Trichel—were not only an indispensable part of what the Ohio State Buckeyes did in 2014, but they are also my go-to guys whom I have counted on time and again, and I have never been disappointed. Coach Mick is the best in his field and has been an invaluable member of my staff for many years. I trust him to the utmost and am fortunate to call him my friend. Tim Kight has had a profound impact on me as both adviser and friend. He is a tremendous source of wisdom, and I learn something new every time I am around him. David Trichel's title at OSU is director of postproduction, but his creativity and influence in our program stretches far beyond his position. Tim and David worked tirelessly, and under a very tight deadline, to ensure that the book was the best it could be.

The first and most important lesson I ever learned from my late parents, Bud and Gisela Meyer, is that there is nothing more sacred or powerful than love of family.

245

ACKNOWLEDGMENTS

I am honored to be the brother of two great sisters, Gigi Escoe and Erika Judd.

My children, Nicki, Gigi, and Nate, make me proud to be their father every day.

My wife, Shelley, has been the love of my life through our twenty-six years of marriage—the greatest source of love, strength, and devotion you can imagine. God has blessed me in more ways than I can count, and with my family most of all.

Urban Meyer

Columbus, Ohio

2014 ROSTER

||||||||||||||||||||||||||||||||||

The 2014 Ohio State team was one of the most selfless groups of people I have ever had the opportunity to coach. Despite the hardships we faced, they kept working and believing in the plan. I am forever grateful to the young men of this team.

ELI APPLE	JACOBY BOREN
DARRYL BALDWIN	JOEY BOSA
WARREN BALL	NOAH BROWN
J. T. BARRETT	JOE BURGER
MARCUS BAUGH	CAM BURROWS
VONN BELL	PARRIS CAMPBELL
MICHAEL BENNETT	MICHAEL CIBENE
KYLE BERGER	JAMES CLARK
DEVAN BOGARD	KYLE CLINTON
DANTE BOOKER	STEPHEN COLLIER

2014 ROSTER

GAREON CONLEY	JEFFIE JOHNSON
JUSTIN COOK	CAMERON JOHNSTON
TAYLOR DECKER	CARDALE JONES
JOHNNIE DIXON	JAMARCO JONES
RUSSELL DOUP	DEMETRIUS KNOX
BRI'ONTE DUNN	MARSHON LATTIMORE
PAT ELFLEIN	MICHAEL LAWLESS
EZEKIEL ELLIOTT	DARRON LEE
CRAIG FADA	TYQUAN LEWIS
CHASE FARRIS	EVAN LISLE
GUY FERRELLI	MIKE MADUKO
CHRIS FONG	JALIN MARSHALL
TREVON FORTE	AARON MAWHIRTER
KHALEED FRANKLIN	DEVLIN MCDANIEL
RASHAD FRAZIER	TERRY MCLAURIN
LOGAN GASKEY	RAEKWON MCMILLAN
JOHN GLESSER	BRAXTON MILLER
CURTIS GRANT	STEVE MILLER
DORAN GRANT	KATO MITCHELL
JEFF GREENE	LUKE MORGAN
PETER GWILYM	R. J. MORRIS
JOEL HALE	DONOVAN MUNGER
BRYCE HAYNES	KEVIN NIEHOFF
JEFF HEUERMAN	SEAN NUERNBERGER
MICHAEL HILL	AARON PARRY
JALYN HOLMES	JOSHUA PERRY
MALIK HOOKER	TYVIS POWELL
SAM HUBBARD	BILLY PRICE

2014 ROSTER

JOE RAMSTETTER

ARMANI REEVES

CHRIS ROCK

JAKE RUSSELL

CURTIS SAMUEL

NIK SARAC

ALEX SCHUSTER

TOMMY SCHUTT

TIM SCOTT

DARIUS SLADE

COREY SMITH

DEVIN SMITH

ERICK SMITH

NICK SNYDER

EVAN SPENCER

TRACY SPRINKLE

RON TANNER

BRADY TAYLOR

NICK TENSING

MICHAEL THOMAS

DYLAN THOMPSON

KYLE TROUT

ZACH TURNURE

ANTONIO UNDERWOOD

NICK VANNETT

ADOLPHUS WASHINGTON

DAMON WEBB

CAM WILLIAMS

ISAIAH WILLIAMS

DONTRE WILSON

CHRIS WORLEY

SAM YORK

ETHAN ZUCAL

IMAGE CREDITS

||||||||||||||||||||||||||||||||||||

IMAGE CREDITS

Insert page 11, below (Art 25): Jonathan Quilter/*The Columbus Dispatch*
Insert page 12, above (Art 26): Kirk Irwin
Insert page 12, below (Art 27): Jonathan Quilter/*The Columbus Dispatch*
Insert page 13, above (Art 28): Kyle Robertson/*The Columbus Dispatch*
Insert page 13, below (Art 29): Jim Davidson for theOzone.net
Insert page 14 (Art 30): Jonathan Quilter/*The Columbus Dispatch*
Insert page 15, above (Art 31): Jonathan Quilter/*The Columbus Dispatch*
Insert page 15, below (Art 32): Jonathan Quilter/*The Columbus Dispatch*
Insert page 16, above (Art 33): Dan Harker for theOzone.net
Insert page 16, below (Art 34): Kyle Robertson/*The Columbus Dispatch*
Insert page 17, above (Art 35): Eamon Queeney/*The Columbus Dispatch*
Insert page 17, below (Art 36): Jonathan Quilter/*The Columbus Dispatch*
Insert page 18, above (Art 37): Dan Harker for theOzone.net
Insert page 18, below (Art 38): Jim Davidson for theOzone.net
Insert page 19 (Art 39): Kyle Robertson/*The Columbus Dispatch*
Insert page 20, above (Art 40): Jim Davidson for theOzone.net
Insert page 20, below (Art 41): Jim Davidson for theOzone.net
Insert page 21, above (Art 42): Jonathan Quilter/*The Columbus Dispatch*
Insert page 21, below (Art 43): Adam Cairns/*The Columbus Dispatch*
Insert page 22 (Art 44): Courtesy of Jeremy Birmingham, elevenwarriors.com
Insert page 23, above (Art 45): Jim Davidson for theOzone.net
Insert page 23, below (Art 46): Brenda Kight
Insert page 24 (Art 47): Kyle Robertson/*The Columbus Dispatch*

INDEX

IIIIIIIIIIIIIIIIIIIIIIIIIIIIIIII

INDEX